Across the Curriculum

with Favorite Authors

Jan Brett

written by Kimberly Suzan Byrd

Illustrated by Agi Palinay

Teacher Created Materials, Inc.
6421 Industry Way
Westminster, CA 92683
www.teachercreated.com

ISBN-1-55734-454-X

©1995 Teacher Created Materials, Inc.
Reprinted, 1999
Made in U.S.A.

The classroom teacher may reproduce copies of materials in this book for classroom use only. The reproduction of any part for an entire school or school system is strictly prohibited. No part of this publication may be transmitted, stored, or recorded in any form without written permission from the publisher.

Table of Contents

Introduction 3

About the Author/Illustrator 4

Literature Web 9

Annotated Bibliography 10

Bibliography 11

Selected Books by Jan Brett

   Goldilocks and the Three Bears (Putnam Publishing, 1990) 12
     (Available in Canada from BeJO Sales, in UK and AUS from World Wide Media)

   Berlioz the Bear (Putnam Publishing, 1991) 24
     (Available in Canada from BeJO Sales, in UK and AUS from World Wide Media)

   The Twelve Days of Christmas (Putnam Publishing, 1986) 32
     (Available in Canada from BeJO Sales, in UK and AUS from World Wide Media)

   The Wild Christmas Reindeer (Putnam Publishing, 1990) 38
     (Available in Canada from BeJO Sales, in UK and AUS from World Wide Media)

   The Mitten: A Ukranian Folktale (Putnam Publishing, 1990) 46
     (Available in Canada from BeJO Sales, in UK and AUS from World Wide Media)

   Annie and the Wild Animals (Houghton Mifflin, 1990) 52
     (Available in Canada from Thomas Allen & Son, in UK from Gollanez Services, in AUS from Jackaranda Wiley)

   The First Dog (Harcourt, Brace, Jovanovich, 1988) 60
     (Available in Canada from HBJ Canada; in UK from HBJ Ltd.; in AUS from HBJ Group, Ltd.)

   The Owl and the Pussycat (Putnam Publishing, 1991) 72
     (Available in Canada from BeJO Sales, in UK and AUS from World Wide Media)

   Trouble with Trolls (Putnam Publishing 1992) 79
     (Available in Canada from BeJo Sales, in UK and AUS from World Wide Media)

   Fritz and the Beautiful Horses (Houghton Mifflin, 1981) 84
     (Available in Canada from Thomas Allen & Son, in UK from Gollanez Services, in AUS from Jackaranda Wiley)

   The Valentine Bears (Houghton Mifflin, 1985) 88
     (Available in Canada from Thomas Allen & Son, in UK from Gollanez Services, in AUS from Jackaranda Wiley)

   The Mother's Day Mice (Houghton Mifflin, 1988) 96
     (Available in Canada from Thomas Allen & Son, in UK from Gollanez Services, in AUS from Jackaranda Wiley)

   Beauty and the Beast (Houghton Mifflin, 1990) 106
     (Available in Canada from Thomas Allen & Son, in UK from Gollanez Services, in AUS from Jackaranda Wiley)

Story Web 108

Venn Diagram 109

Achievement Award 110

Materials and Resources 111

 # 454 Favorite Authors: Jan Brett   2   *© 1995 Teacher Created Materials, Inc.*

Introduction

Our teaching is enriched daily by the wealth of outstanding authors who give us words and pictures to engage, motivate, and inspire our students. Through these authors, our students become acquainted with worlds and ideas beyond their own and emerge as more aware, active, and enthusiastic readers.

In this author series, one author is spotlighted in each resource book. Teachers and students have the opportunity to participate in an in-depth study of each author's work and style. Integrated activities from all curriculum areas are included to make the unit more meaningful to young children.

Curriculum areas highlighted in this unit include the following:

❑ language arts

❑ math

❑ science

❑ art

❑ music

❑ movement

❑ drama

❑ cooking

❑ games

We are confident the author approach to studying literature will be a satisfying experience for you and your students.

About the Author/Illustrator

Jan Brett

Jan Brett has ten independently published books; six are original stories, and four are adaptations of classic literary works. With the exception of *Fritz and the Beautiful Horses*, all of these books include a unique device—detailed border artwork in which an entirely separate story is taking place. Her illustrations are beautiful, whimsical, lavish, and full of life—sure to entice readers. The main purpose of this unit is to encourage young children to listen carefully to stories, use pictures as clues to events that are occurring, retell or dramatize stories, and begin writing their own stories.

About the Author/Illustrator

Jan Brett *(cont.)*

Jan Brett was born in New England on December 1, 1949. She grew up in Massachusetts not far from where she now lives. She decided to become an artist in kindergarten because she loved to draw. As a child, she spent many hours reading and drawing. She is a graduate of Colby-Sawyer College in New Hampshire. Brett also attended the Museum School at the Boston Museum of Fine Arts. She began her art career by creating restaurant menus, greeting cards, and school texts, always with an eye towards writing and illustrating her own children's books.

Jan Brett was a divorced, single mother until she met Joseph Hearne, whom she married in 1981. She dedicated her book *The Owl and the Pussycat* to Lia, her daughter, who is a graduate of Bucknell University. Hearne is a graduate of the Julliard School of Music in New York. He plays double bass for the Boston Symphony Orchestra in addition to airbrushing the backgrounds of Brett's books. Hearne became Brett's inspiration for Berlioz in her story *Berlioz the Bear.*

In her childhood, Brett often retreated into the pages of beautiful picture books and dreamed of becoming an illustrator. "I used to always fantasize about being left on a desert island so I could draw all the time," she once said in an interview with Scholastic Books. She continues, "I remember the special quiet of rainy days when I felt that I could enter the pages of my beautiful picture books. Now I try to recreate that feeling of believing that the imaginary place I'm drawing really exists. The detail in my work helps to convince me, and I hope others as well, that such places might be real."

Brett says her favorite book is whichever one she is currently working on because she feels most like herself when she is drawing. It is easy to see that Brett loves what she does because each of her books reflects her unwavering attention to detail and passion for authenticity. Jan Brett infuses her books with the painstaking care of a master artisan.

Brett is the author/illustrator of six children's books. She has also retold and illustrated three classic tales, an epic poem, and a traditional Christmas counting song. She has illustrated over 15 books for other authors. Her first book, *Fritz and the Beautiful Horses*, received the Parent's Choice award as one of the best children's books for 1981. All told, Jan Brett's books have garnered over 40 awards.

Brett loves to hear from her readers. She welcomes mail from teachers and students and sends replies. She is happy to send elementary educators a "teacher's pack" and her yearly newsletter with detailed information about one of her books. As a courtesy to the author/illustrator, send a single letter from the class when writing or else package individual student letters in a single large envelope and send to the following address.

> Jan Brett
> 132 Pleasant Street
> Norwell, MA 02061

© 1995 Teacher Created Materials, Inc.   *# 454 Favorite Authors: Jan Brett*

About the Author/Illustrator

The Art and Artistry of Jan Brett

Teachers are presented with a wonderful opportunity to enhance children's aesthetic appreciation whenever using Jan Brett's books. Her rich attention to detail will encourage both children and adults to look carefully at the pictures. The background details (landscape, architecture, costumes, etc.) of her books swiftly transport her readers to the region depicted in the story. Brett accurately provides this solid sense of place in each of her books. Her settings are inspired by her imagination (for example, the North Pole, the trolls' underground hideaway, etc.) and her travel experiences (to the Caribbean, Norway, and Bavaria, to name just a few examples). Together with her husband, Brett visits many countries around the world, where she then researches the costumes, architecture, art, and landscapes which appear in her work.

As mentioned before, with the exception of *Fritz and the Beautiful Horses,* all the books written and illustrated by Jan Brett include detailed border artwork in which an entirely separate story is taking place. This distinctive device has become Jan Brett's trademark. She has often stated that she uses the borders when she has too many ideas for one book. Thus, the borders become the showcase for her subplots. In *The Mitten,* the borders show Nicki walking through the woods, scaring the next animal out of its hiding place. The borders of *The Wild Christmas Reindeer* highlight the elves busily making toys, while those in *The Twelve Days of Christmas* feature a family's preparation for the holiday season. In *Annie and the Wild Animals*, we learn of the birth of Taffy's kittens from studying the border pictures. In *Berlioz the Bear*, the borders picture the townspeople gathering for a gala ball. Brett's borders appear on the bottoms of the pages as well as on the sides in *The Owl and the Pussycat.* The love story between two goldfish unfolds in underwater borders while straw mats and flowers indigenous to the Caribbean appear in the side borders. In *Goldilocks and the Three Bears*, the reader follows the bears' progress through the woods, while the borders in *Trouble with Trolls* focus on the hedgehog making his way to the underground hideaway.

Jan Brett's inventive use of borders is an excellent way to acquaint children with subplots and foreshadowing. The illustrations often hint at what will occur in the main story. Teachers should provide plenty of opportunities for children to predict what will happen before turning the page and continuing with the story.

 # 454 Favorite Authors: Jan Brett   *© 1995 Teacher Created Materials, Inc.*

About the Author/Illustrator

Illustration Technique

Jan Brett first draws a pencil or pen-and-ink sketch. Then she uses watercolors to paint the characters and settings. She prefers a fine, almost dry, brush, using this technique to prevent the colors from running together. It takes Brett an hour to paint one square inch. That adds up to about a week to watercolor one page, a rate of progress which means an average of four or five months for each book.

Young children can imitate Jan Brett's illustration style. Some ideas for recreating her technique include the following:

◆ Have children paint a picture with watercolors. Mount their paintings behind a heart stencil mat. Encourage them to decorate the mat with colored pasta, glitter, seashells, pine cones, etc.

◆ Directions for tinting pasta: Place one tablespoon (15 mL) of rubbing alcohol and a few drops of desired food coloring into a large resealable plastic bag with a box/bag of pasta. Shake well. Spread pasta onto waxed paper until dry (10–15 minutes).

◆ Ask the children to paint pictures in the medium of their choice (watercolor, dry tempera, crayon resist, etc.). Mount their paintings on construction paper, being sure to leave a 2" (5 cm) border on each side. Encourage children to create designs in the borders with chalk, markers, glitter, etc.

◆ Encourage the children to draw pictures. Mount their illustrations on construction paper, being sure to leave a 2" (5 cm) border on each side. Allow children to decorate their borders with rubber stamp designs (bears, bees, cats, Christmas items, reindeer, owls, seashells, fish, trolls, dogs, hearts, mice, etc.). Older children can add a three-dimensional look and texture to their borders by using a stamping technique known as embossing.

◆ Ask the entire class to brainstorm a story idea (you will need a main plot and a subplot). Write the story as a group, with each child contributing one idea. When the story is ready to be illustrated, each child should complete the page containing his/her idea. Each drawing should include border artwork which furthers the subplot. Older children will be able to complete their own story on an individual basis.

© 1995 Teacher Created Materials, Inc.　　　　7　　　　# 454 Favorite Authors: Jan Brett

About the Author/Illustrator

Author/Illustrator Chart

Teachers can create a wall chart to highlight important information about author/illustrator Jan Brett. Write the following facts on 1" (2.5 cm) ruled chart paper from a 24" x 32" (60 cm x 80 cm) tablet (available at most teacher supply stores):

Write information on the chart in black marker, being sure to highlight Jan Brett's name by using another color. Attach a photograph of Jan Brett to the chart where indicated (she usually includes one with the "teacher's pack" she mails educators). Purchase a paperback version of one of her books or a calendar (published yearly and available at most book stores) featuring her artwork. Use these illustrations on the wall chart where indicated.

Literature Web

The Owl and the Pussycat
Trouble with Trolls
Fritz and the Beautiful Horses
The Valentine Bears
The Mother's Day Mice
Beauty and the Beast

Berlioz the Bear
The Twelve Days of Christmas
The Wild Christmas Reindeer
The Mitten: A Ukranian Folktale
Annie and the Wild Animals
The First Dog

Music
singing/musical/patterns
playing instruments
listening to various forms of music
orchestra information

Cooking
mixing   eating
baking   timing
rolling   math/science concepts
measuring

Games
recall
verbal skills
visual discrimination
listening skills
fun

Jan Brett

Language Arts
listening/writing/dictating
Bloom's taxonomy of skills
other languages
rhyming/poetry
Goldilocks and the Three Bears

Math/Science
classification/sets   ordinal numbers
patterning/seriating   matching/sorting
planting/growing   observing
seasons/calendar   experimenting
graphing/counting   studying animals

Drama
dramatizing stories
simple debate
panel discussion
circle-story drama
encouraging imagination

Art
creating   weaving
print making   gluing
painting   drawing
cutting   illustrating
lacing   sculpting

© 1995 Teacher Created Materials, Inc.   9   # 454 Favorite Authors: Jan Brett

Annotated Bibliography

(works included in this book)

Annie and the Wild Animals. Houghton Mifflin Company, 1985. When Annie's cat disappears, she tries to locate a new pet.

Beauty and the Beast. Clarion, 1989. A kind and beautiful maid's love releases a handsome prince from the spell that has made him an ugly beast.

Berlioz the Bear. G.P. Putnam's Sons, 1991. Berlioz and his fellow musicians are due to play for the town ball when their wagon becomes stuck in a hole. A bee helps save the day.

The First Dog. Harcourt Brace Jovanovich, 1988. In this exciting tale of adventure in prehistoric times, Paleowolf befriends Kip the cave boy and becomes the first dog.

Fritz and the Beautiful Horses. Houghton Mifflin Company, 1981. Fritz, a pony excluded from the group of beautiful horses within the walled city, becomes a hero when he rescues the children of the city.

Goldilocks and the Three Bears. Putnam Publishing, 1987. An adventuresome little girl enters an unoccupied cottage and wreaks havoc on its contents.

The Mitten: A Ukranian Folktale. G.P. Putnam's Sons, 1989. A Ukrainian folktale in which a variety of animals squeeze into a little boy's lost mitten.

The Mother's Day Mice. Clarion, 1986. Three little mice go to the meadow in search of the perfect Mother's Day presents, but it is the littlest mouse who discovers the most unusual gift of all.

The Owl and the Pussycat. G.P. Putnam's, 1991. After a courtship of a year and a day, Owl and Pussycat are married.

Trouble with Trolls. G.P. Putnam's Sons, 1992. While climbing Mt. Baldy, Treve outwits some trolls who want to make her dog their pet.

The Twelve Days of Christmas. G.P. Putnam's Sons, 1986. A young woman's true love sends her extravagant gifts on each of the twelve days of Christmas.

The Valentine Bears. Clarion, 1983. Mr. and Mrs. Bear celebrate their first Valentine's Day together.

The Wild Christmas Reindeer. G.P. Putnam's Sons, 1990. After a few false starts, Teeka discovers the best way to prepare Santa's reindeer for Christmas Eve.

Bibliography

Books Written and Illustrated by Jan Brett

Annie and the Wild Animals (Houghton Mifflin, 1990)

Berlioz the Bear (Putnam Publishing, 1991)

Fritz and the Beautiful Horses (Houghton Mifflin, 1981)

The Wild Christmas Reindeer (Putnam Publishing, 1990)

The First Dog (Harcourt Brace Jovanovich, 1988)

Trouble with Trolls (Putnam Publishing, 1992)

Books Retold and Illustrated by Jan Brett

Beauty and the Beast (Houghton Mifflin, 1990)

Goldilocks and the Three Bears (Putnam Publishing, 1987)

The Mitten: A Ukranian Folktale (Putnam Publishing, 1989)

Books Illustrated by Jan Brett

Happy Birthday, Dear Duck (Clarion, 1988)

In the Castle of Cats (Dutton, 1981)

Inside a Sand Castle (Houghton Mifflin, 1979)

Look at the Kittens (Random House, 1987)

Noelle of the Nutcracker (Houghton Mifflin, 1986)

Old Devil Is Waiting (Harcourt Brace Jovanovich, 1985)

Scary, Scary Halloween (Houghton Mifflin, 1988)

Secret Clocks (Viking Press, 1979)

Some Birds Have Funny Names (Crown, 1983)

St. Patrick's Day in the Morning (Houghton Mifflin, 1983)

The Mother's Day Mice (Houghton Mifflin, 1988)

The Enchanted Book (Harcourt Brace Jovanovich, 1987)

The Twelve Days of Christmas (Putnam Publishing, 1986)

The Owl and the Pussycat (Putnam Publishing, 1991)

The Valentine Bears (Houghton Mifflin, 1985)

Where Are all the Kittens? (Random House, 1984)

Woodland Crossings (Atheneum, 1978)

Young Melvin and Bulger (Doubleday, 1981)

© 1995 Teacher Created Materials, Inc.   *# 454 Favorite Authors: Jan Brett*

Goldilocks and the Three Bears

This story was an editor's choice for *Booklist* and voted best book of the year by *Newsweek* and *Parents* magazines. One of Jan Brett's pets, Little Pearl, was the model for the mouse in the story. The model for Goldilocks was an adventuresome little girl named Miriam. Folklore and fairy tales have captured the imagination of Jan Brett since she was a little girl. In her interpretation of this beloved tale, she showcases several of her trademarks—traditional European costuming, a resilient and resourceful heroine, brilliant border artwork, and animals so real you can practically see their whiskers twitch, thus making this the perfect book to begin an author/illustrator study of Jan Brett.

Language Arts

1. Read *Goldilocks and the Three Bears*. Lead children in a discussion about Goldilocks' curiosity and adventuresome nature. Would they enter an unoccupied cottage? Why or why not?

2. Story-Within-a-Story Device—Show children the illustrations again. If possible, project them onto a screen using an opaque projector. In each illustration, locate and discuss the mouse/mice shown. Talk about the separate story involving the mice.

3. Retelling the Story—Allow children to retell this timeless tale using either the flannelboard set from The Story Teller (1-800-272-5641) or wooden magnets from Childwood (1-206-842-3472).

4. Fingerplay—The Three Bears

   This is Mama Bear, as nice as can be,

   This is Papa Bear, the biggest is he,

   This is Baby Bear, he's growing up tall,

   He likes little things because he's small.

5. Story Sequence—Have children sequence pictures of the story events. Copy, color, cut out, and laminate page 15.

6. Writing Stories—Have children write about the Three Bears' visit to Goldilocks' house.

7. Bloom's Taxonomy of Higher Order Questions:

   Knowledge—What was the little girl's name?

   What did Goldilocks do to the porridge?

   Comprehension—Why did Goldilocks eat Baby Bear's porridge?

   Why were there three bowls on the table?

   Application—What do you do when your cereal is too hot?

   If Goldilocks came to your house, what would she find to eat?

   Analysis—What parts of the story could not have happened?

   List three differences between Papa Bear's cereal and Baby Bear's cereal.

   Synthesis—How would the story be different if Goldilocks visited three fish?

   How would it have changed the story if the Three Bears had been at home?

   Evaluation—Do you think Goldilocks was good or bad? Why?

   Was Goldilocks smart to go into an unoccupied cottage?

Goldilocks and the Three Bears *(cont.)*

Math/Science

1. Three Bear Family Counters by Learning Resources (available at most teacher supply stores)—Children sort bears by size (large/Papa, medium/Mama, small/Baby), weight, or color (red, yellow, blue, and green).

2. Baby Bear's Quilt Patterns—Enlarge the pattern on page 16 and mount it on poster board. Attach two to three rows of Velcro-backed plastic hooks below the pattern, approximately 2" (5 cm) apart. Cut a variety of colored poster board into 1 1/2" x 1 1/2" (3.75 cm x 3.75 cm) squares. Punch a hole in the middle of one side near the top edge. Start a pattern by hanging the colored squares from the hooks—for example, pink, blue, pink, blue, etc., and allow children to complete it. As they become more proficient, increase the difficulty of the pattern—for example, red, blue, pink, yellow, red, blue, pink, yellow, etc.

3. Classification—Have children sort objects and/or pictures into big/small, hot/cold, and hard/soft categories, using activity sheets on pages 17–19.

4. Sets of Three—Have children group items into sets of three (bowls, spoons, beds, bears, etc.). Discuss small, medium, and large, as well as ordinal numbers (first, second, and third).

5. Little Bear's Clothes Match—Have children match numeral on shirt to number of objects on shorts. Trace patterns from pages 20–21 onto poster board or tagboard. Program shirts with numbers 1–10 (or 11–20 for older students). Program shorts with the corresponding number of objects. Laminate bears and clothes. Attach Velcro where indicated on patterns.

6. Planting Crocuses—Determine the sequence of planting and tending crocuses from border pictures. Provide supplies for children to plant their own.

Art

1. Goldilocks' Kitchen Gadget Prints—Children make prints using utensils Goldilocks may have found in the Three Bears' kitchen—for example, egg beater, wire mesh strainer, potato masher, pastry brush, cookie cutter, tea infuser, etc. Discuss the different kitchen utensils and what they are used for in cooking.

2. Story Border Pictures—(The child draws a picture—a scene from the story or a completely unrelated scene.) Place construction paper mat around the picture and encourage the child to decorate this border as Jan Brett often does in her books.

Music

1. *Goldilocks and the Three Bears* story with kazoos (See page 22.)

2. "Three Brown Bears" song in *Totline Theme-A-Saurus* (See page 111.)

3. "Baby Bear's Chicken Pox" on *Sniggles, Squirrels, and Chicken Pox* by Miss Jackie Weisman and Friends (great for preschoolers during chicken pox epidemics!) See page 112.

© 1995 Teacher Created Materials, Inc.   13   *# 454 Favorite Authors: Jan Brett*

Goldilocks and the Three Bears *(cont.)*

Drama

1. Act out the story using props.
2. Panel Discussion—Goldilocks is accused of wrecking the bears' cottage. Panel members consist of "individuals who know Goldilocks and the Three Bears" and speak on their behalf.
3. Goldilocks: The Trial—Guilty or Not?

Children debate the innocence or guilt of Goldilocks. Upon completion, share the book *Deep in the Forest* by Brinton Turkle with students. In this version, Baby Bear trashes Goldilock's house. Ask children to tell which version of the folktale they believe and why. Presenting both versions allows children to formulate their own opinions about the truth and to see that there are almost always two sides to an issue.

Cooking

Bear Porridge

Mix two cups (500 mL) of quick oats with four cups (1 L) of water and 3/4 teaspoon (3.75 mL) salt. Stir oats into rapidly boiling water. Boil one minute, stirring occasionally. Cook oatmeal longer for smoother texture (if desired). For thicker oatmeal, use less water. For thinner oatmeal, use more water.

Yield: six 2/3 cup (170 mL) servings

Bear Sugar Cookies

(If no oven is available at school, use the No-Bake Chocolate Oatmeal cookies below.)

Use prepared sugar cookie dough. Follow directions for rolling out dough. Let students cut out their own bears with a bear cookie cutter (available in most houseware departments). Let the students decorate their own cookies with raisins, sprinkles, chocolate chips, etc. Bake according to directions and enjoy with milk or punch after lunch.

No-Bake Chocolate Oatmeal Cookies

2 cups (500 mL) sugar

1/2 cup (125 mL) butter or margarine

1/2 cup (125 mL) canned milk

Mix and boil three minutes, stirring constantly. Remove from heat.

Stir in the following ingredients:

1 cup (250 mL) small marshmallows

1/2 cup (125 mL) sifted cocoa powder

3 cups (750 mL) quick oats

Drop at once on waxed paper. Work fast while mixture is hot; it hardens quickly as it cools. The yield is about three dozen.

 # 454 Favorite Authors: Jan Brett

Goldilocks and the Three Bears

Story Sequence Cards

© 1995 Teacher Created Materials, Inc.   15   #454 Favorite Authors: Jan Brett

Goldilocks and the Three Bears

Baby Bear's Quilt Patterns

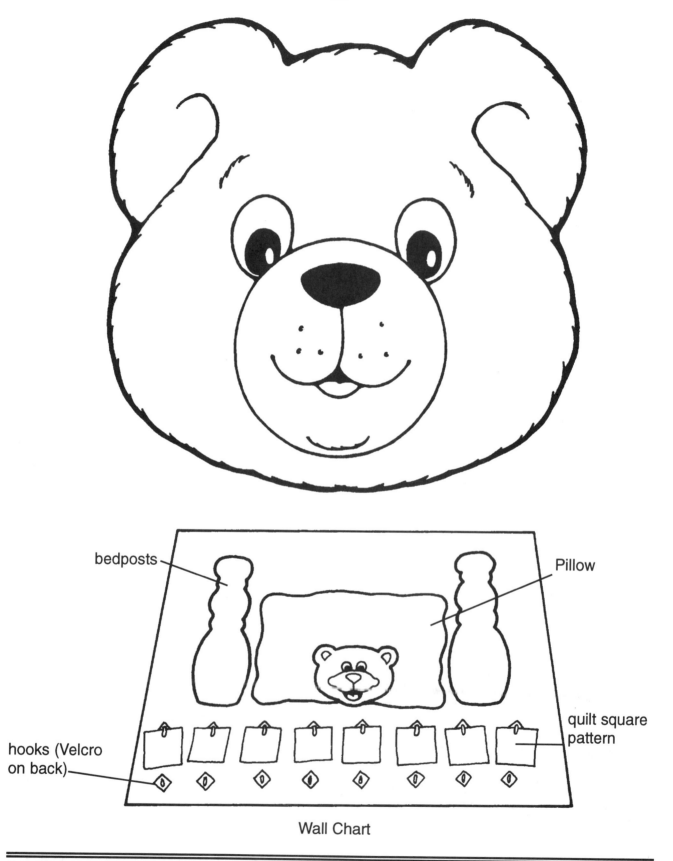

Wall Chart

#454 Favorite Authors: Jan Brett © 1995 Teacher Created Materials, Inc.

Goldilocks and the Three Bears

Big/Small Classification

As BIG as papa Bear

As small as Baby Bear

Goldilocks and the Three Bears

Hot/Cold Classification

As hot as Papa's porridge

As cold as Mama's porridge

Hard/Soft Classification

As hard as Papa's Bed

As soft as Mama's Chair

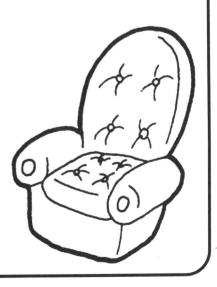

Goldilocks and the Three Bears

Baby Bear's Clothes Match

Teacher's Note: Place a Velcro tab on the back of each piece of clothing. Align matching tabs on bear (page 21) so that the shirt and pants will fit correctly when attached to the bear pattern.

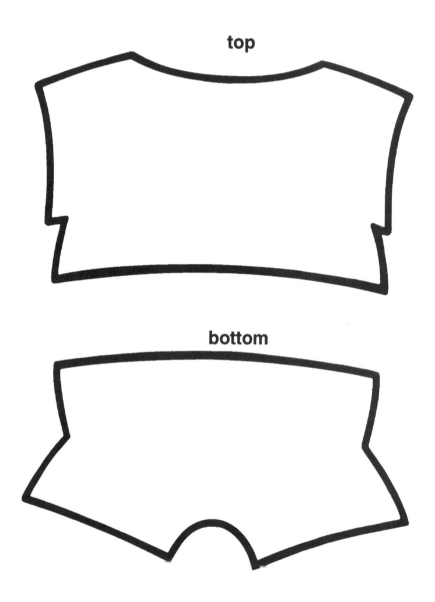

top

bottom

Goldilocks and the Three Bears

Baby Bear's Clothes Match (cont.)

Teacher's Note: Place Velcro tabs in positions to allow matching clothes pieces from page 20 to be placed correctly.

Goldilocks and the Three Bears

Goldilocks and the Three Bears with Kazoos

Practice the following sounds (using kazoos) with the children: *going up stairs, three knocks, squeaky door, ouch!, brr! mmm!, uh oh!, rocking chair, rocking fast, creaky bed, snore, growl, running down stairs,* and *running*.

Once upon a time there were three bears. Their porridge was too hot, so they decided to go for a walk. Along came Goldilocks. She went up the stairs *(steps)* to the porch and knocked on the door three times *(knock, knock, knock)*. She opened the door *(creak)* and went right in. First, she tried Papa Bear's porridge, but it was too hot *(ouch!)*. Next, she tried Mama Bear's porridge, but it was too cold *(brr!)*. Then she tried Baby Bear's porridge and it was just right *(mmm!)*. So Goldilocks ate it all up, and the bowl fell off the table and onto the floor and broke *(uh oh!)*.

Goldilocks went into the living room to sit down. First, she tried Papa Bear's chair, but it was too hard *(ouch!)*. Next, she tried Mama Bear's chair, but it was too soft *(mmm!)*. Then she tried Baby Bear's chair *(rocking)*, and it was just right. So Goldilocks rocked faster and faster *(rocking)* until the chair broke in two *(uh oh!)*.

Goldilocks went upstairs *(steps)*. First, she tried Papa Bear's bed *(creak)*, but it too hard *(ouch!)*. Next, she tried Mama Bear's bed *(creak)*, but it was too soft *(mmm!)*. Then she tried Baby Bear's bed *(creak)*, and it was just right, so she curled up and went sound asleep *(snore)*.

Meanwhile, the three bears came back home. They saw the porridge and the chairs and went upstairs *(steps)*. There they saw Goldilocks in Baby Bear's bed. Papa Bear growled *(grrr!)* and Goldilocks woke up. She was so afraid that she ran downstairs, opened the door *(squeak)*, slammed the door and ran *(fast steps)* all the way home. As for the three bears, they never saw Goldilocks again.

Invitation

Please join us for a presentation of
Goldilocks and the Three Bears

by

_____

on this date and this time

_____

at this place

_____

Berlioz the Bear

This Reading Rainbow book is dedicated to Joseph Hearne, who airbrushes the backgrounds of Jan Brett's books with a fine spray of paint. But Joseph Hearne is much more than Jan Brett's artistic associate. He is her husband and the model for Berlioz. Hearne is also a bassist for the Boston Symphony Orchestra. One day Brett asked her husband if the tone of his double bass changed with the weather. He told her that the instrument was over 100 years old and sometimes the wood dried out and cracked, causing a buzzing sound to come from the bass. At that moment, Brett came up with the idea of putting a bee inside Berlioz's double bass.

Berlioz (BEAR-LEE-OZE: the last part rhymes with *toes*) is named after the French composer, Hector Berlioz. Jan Brett loves to listen to classical music, and her favorite piece by Berlioz is "The Hungarian March."

Brett wanted each of the musicians in *Berlioz the Bear* to have a distinctive personality, so she asked five other members of the Boston Symphony Orchestra to pose for her. Tom Martin, who is tall, lanky, and droll, became the bear who plays clarinet. The handsome blond drummer, Tom Gauger, became the model for the percussionist. Brett chose Martha Babcock, a cellist, because she was elegant and thoughtful. Brett did not want Berlioz's bass upstaged by a cello, so she changed the instrument to a French horn. Brett describes Martha's violinist husband, Harvey Siegel, as "unflappable," which explains why the violinist in *Berlioz the Bear* is reading the entire time the bandwagon is stuck in the hole. Norman Bolter became the model for the trombone player. Brett wanted to use him because his eyebrows were so expressive.

The Boston Symphony Orchestra often travels to Europe on tour. A recent trip to Bavaria inspired the scenes and costumes for this story. Jan Brett and Joseph Hearne happened upon a May Day concert and celebration in Grunwald, where the townspeople were dressed in traditional costumes—lederhosen (leather pants) for the men and dirndls (full-skirted dresses) for the women. The characters in *Berlioz the Bear* sport these traditional German costumes. On the last day of their trip at a folk art museum in the village of Bad Tolz, Brett and Hearne located the bandwagon that became the model for the one in the story. *Berlioz the Bear* is a logical choice to follow up a study of *Goldilocks and the Three Bears* or to serve as an introduction to a unit on music.

Language Arts

1. Read *Berlioz the Bear*. Ask students to guess what musical piece Berlioz played as an encore. Play a recording of Rimsky-Korsakov's "Flight of the Bumblebee" and have students pretend to be bumblebees while the music plays.

2. Predicting   Ask the children to predict or guess what is inside of Berlioz's instrument. Encourage them to predict what is going to happen in the story, using the main story as well as the picture clues in the border subplot.

 # 454 Favorite Authors: Jan Brett   24   *© 1995 Teacher Created Materials, Inc.*

Berlioz the Bear (cont.)

Language Arts (cont.)

3. Fingerplay—Bees

    A. Bees

    Here is the beehive,
    Where are the bees?
    Hidden away where nobody sees.
    Soon they'll be coming out of the hive,
    1, 2, 3, 4, 5!

    B. Five Little Bees

    One little bee flew and flew,
    He met a friend and that made two.
    Two little bees, busy as could be,
    Along came another, and that made three.
    Three little bees wanted one more,
    They found one soon, and that made four.
    Four little bees, going to the hive,
    Spied their little brother, and that made five.
    Five little bees working every hour,
    Buzz away bees and find another flower!

4. Bloom's Taxonomy of Higher Order Questions:

    Knowledge—Name all of the animals that tried to help the mule pull the wagon out of the hole.

    What was making the buzzing noise inside the double bass?

    Comprehension—What caused the mule to finally move?

    Application—If you were Berlioz, what would you have done to get the bandwagon out of the hole?

    Analysis—Compare the mule and the plowhorse. How are they alike? How are they different?

    Synthesis—How would the story have changed if the bee had not stung the mule?

    Evaluation—Do you think Berlioz's choice of an encore was appropriate? Why or why not?

Math/Science

1. Patterns—Discuss the fact that music often has repeated notes and rests. Clap patterns to familiar tunes. Use "Clap and Rest" on *The Feel of Music* by Hap Palmer and "Play and Rest" on *Homemade Band* by Hap Palmer.

2. Graphing—Graph favorite types of music (following music activity #2).

3. Bees and Honey—Discuss the bee community (queen, drone, worker, guard) and each one's job in the hive. Show the children a beehive. Invite a beekeeper to explain how bees make honey. Use a faceted magnifying viewer to simulate a bee's eye. Allow children to look through the viewer and describe what they see.

    An excellent source for factual information and pictures of bees is *Honeybees* by Barrie Watts.

4. Bee Diagram—Children label the bee diagram on page 29. Copy the page for each child in your class. A labeled diagram appears on page 30.

Berlioz the Bear (cont.)

Math/Science (cont.)

5. Honeybee Facts—Share the following information about bees with the class:
    - Bees are insects having three body parts, two antennae, and six legs.
    - Bees' body parts consist of head, thorax, and abdomen.
    - Bees have five eyes (two compound, three simple).
    - The queen bee's job is to lay eggs.
    - The drone's job is to fertilize the queen.
    - The worker bee's job is to take care of the hive, nurse the larvae, and gather pollen and nectar.
    - The guard's job is to protect the hive.
    - A bee's wings create the buzzing sound we hear.
    - Only one queen bee lives in each hive.

Art

1. Make musical instruments (for example, kazoos from toilet paper rolls, wax paper, and rubber bands; drums from oatmeal boxes; shakers from film canisters; tambourines from aluminum pie pans, etc.).
2. Bee Flight—Children use watercolors to create the path a bee takes during his flight while listening to different versions of "Flight of the Bumblebee" (pre-writing skill). Copy page 31 for each child in the class.
3. Honeycombs—Children create a hive using Honeycomb cereal. Simply allow children to glue cereal shapes to poster board to form a hive. Yellow pompon "bees" can be glued inside a cell.
4. Bees in Honeycombs—Children can glue empty toilet paper tubes together to create a hive (lay them lengthwise to glue together). Eraser bees can be purchased from a novelty store. Give each child five bees to act out the fingerplay "Bees."

Music

1. "Flight of the Bumblebee"—see Language Arts activity #1 and Art activity #2.
2. Listen to various types of music, such as classical, jazz, rhythm and blues, contemporary, country, rock, rap, etc.
3. Play instruments to "Slow and Fast" and "Soft and Loud" on *Homemade Band* by Hap Palmer.
4. Song

   "Buzzin' Round the Hive"
   (tune: "She'll Be Comin' 'Round the Mountain")
   Oh, the honeybees are buzzin' 'round the hive, Buzz! Buzz!
   Oh, the honeybees are buzzin' 'round the hive, Buzz! Buzz!
   Oh, the honeybees are buzzin' oh, the honeybees are buzzin',
   Oh, the honeybees are buzzin' 'round the hive, Buzz! Buzz!

5. Orchestra—Set up the circle to represent an orchestra arrangement. Ask parent volunteers to come in and play instruments. Borrow instruments for children to play. Discuss the different groups within the orchestra (woodwinds, percussion, horns, strings, etc.). Show pictures of instruments if real ones are unavailable for classroom use. Play music and identify the different instruments as they are heard.

 # 454 Favorite Authors: Jan Brett

Berlioz the Bear (cont.)

Music (cont.)

6. Song

    "Baby Bumblebee"
    (tune: "Arkansas Traveler")
    Oh, I'm bringing home a baby bumblebee,
    Won't my mommy be so proud of me,
    I'm bringing home a baby bumblebee,
    OUCH!! It stung me! (spoken)
    I'm squishing up the baby bumblebee,
    Won't my mommy be so proud of me,
    I'm squishing up the baby bumblebee,
    Ooooh, it's yucky! (spoken)
    I'm wiping off the baby bumblebee,
    Won't my mommy be so proud of me,
    I'm wiping off the baby bumblebee,
    Now my mommy won't be mad at me! (spoken)

7. Musical Chairs

    Every child sits in a chair. As music is being played, the children walk around the circle of chairs. The teacher removes a few chairs at a time. Stop the music and allow children to locate empty chairs. Those left standing are excused to go to another activity. Continue play until only one child is left.

8. **"I Wanna Be a Friend of Yours"**

    (The tune for this song and an associated circle dance are contained in *Musical Games for Children of All Ages,* by Esther L. Nelson, Sterling Publishing Co., Inc., 1976.)

    I wanna be a friend of yours, mmmm and a little bit more.
    I wanna be a pal of yours, mmmm and a little bit more.
    I wanna be a bumblebee,
    Buzzing round your door.
    I wanna mean a lot to you,
    Mmmm and little bit more, mmmm and a little bit,
    Mmmm and whole lot more.
    Oh, you are a friend of mine, mmmm and a little bit more.
    You are a pal of mine, mmmm and a little bit more.
    You are a bumblebee,
    Buzzing round my door.
    You mean a lot to me,
    Mmmm and a little bit,
    Mmmm and a little bit,
    Mmmm and a whole lot more.

9. Field Trip

    Attend a symphony or orchestra performance geared towards young children.

10. Video—Disney's *Peter and the Wolf*

Berlioz the Bear (cont.)

Games

Bear Bag Toss

Cut holes from a large cardboard bear or bear head for a bean-bag toss. Assign points to each hole. Hang between two chairs. Students take turns tossing small bean bags at the target. An adult or upper grade student may keep score.

Bears in the Den

Adapt the children's game Squirrel in the Tree. Divide the class into groups of three. Two children join hands to form a "den." A third child is the "bear" inside the den. There should be one or two extra children. When the leader shouts, "Spring," the bears leave their dens and join the extra children to run around the playing area. If "summer" or "fall" is called, the bears continue to run around outside the dens. When "winter" is called, each bear must find a new den. Bears left without a den must leave the game. A new round begins with one of the den groups becoming the extra children.

Cooking

Edible Dough Bumblebees

    1 cup (250 mL) peanut butter
    1/2 cup (125 mL) honey
    1 1/2 cups (375 mL) powdered milk

Mix ingredients together and mold into bee-shaped body. Add two banana slices for wings and two raisin eyes.

Berlioz's Honey Bee Cookies

    2 1/4 cups (563 mL) sifted flour
    1 teaspoon (5 mL) baking soda
    1/4 teaspoon (1 mL) salt
    1/2 teaspoon (2 mL) cinnamon
    1/2 cup (125 mL) softened butter or margarine
    1 cup (250 mL) honey
    1/2 cup (125 mL) brown sugar
    2 eggs, well beaten
    1 1/2 (375 mL) cups raisins
    1/2 cup (125 mL) chopped walnuts

Sift flour, soda, salt, and spices together. Cream butter and brown sugar. Stir honey into creamed mixture. Add eggs, then dry ingredients. Stir in raisins and nuts. Mix thoroughly. Drop from teaspoon onto a greased baking sheet. Bake at 350° F (180° C) for 12–15 minutes.

Yield: 4 dozen

Bee Diagram

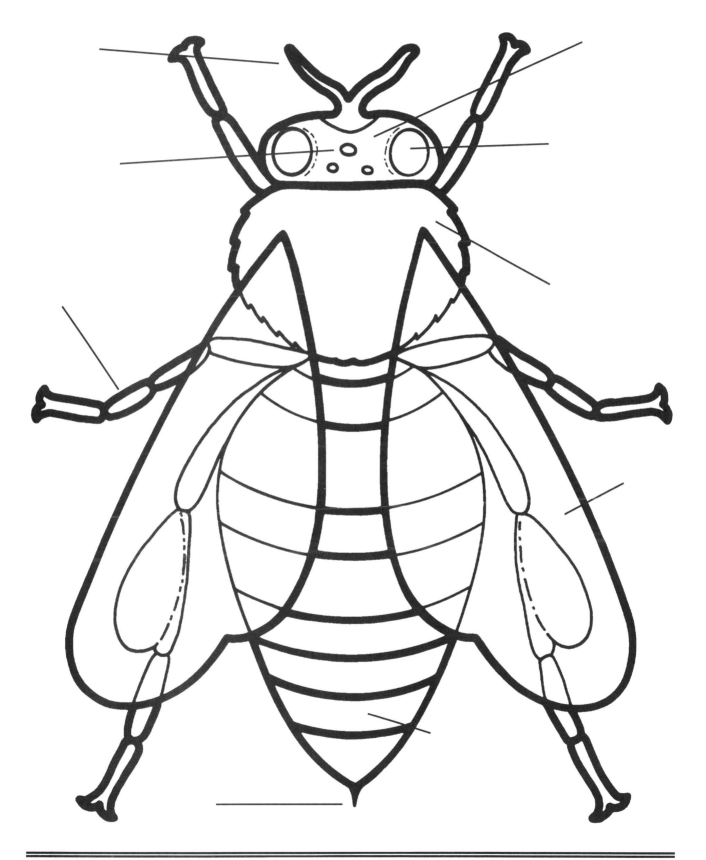

Labeled Bee Diagram

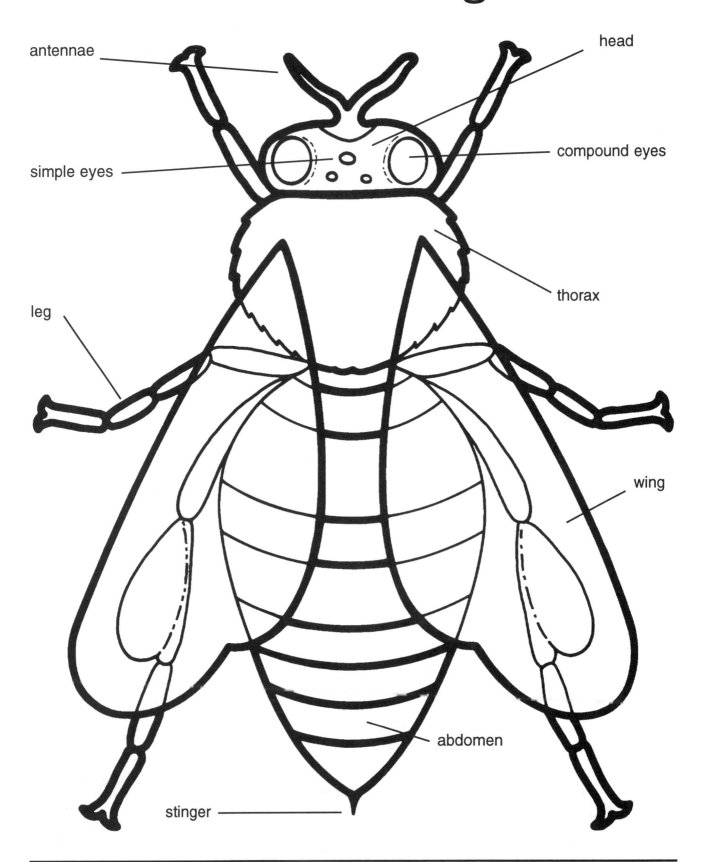

Watercolor Flight of the Bumblebee

The Twelve Days Of Christmas

Hoping to inject new vibrancy into a traditional English carol, Jan Brett created her own version of "The Twelve Days of Christmas." The border artwork on 11 of the two-page spreads contains the words "Merry Christmas" written in different languages. When reading the book to children, be sure to mention that the artist whimsically sees herself as the goose in the white babushka in the illustration for "Six geese a-laying." *The Twelve Days of Christmas* can be combined with *The Wild Christmas Reindeer, The Mitten,* and *Annie and the Wild Animals* during the month of December as a winter/holiday unit completely independent of this author study. *The Twelve Days of Christmas* was an editor's choice for *Booklist* magazine.

Language Arts

1. Read *The Twelve Days of Christmas.* Explain vocabulary as necessary—for example, partridge, turtledoves, colly birds (an English dialect word for "blackbirds"), lords, etc.

2. Foreign Language Study—Have children learn to say "Merry Christmas" in the 11 different languages contained in the border artwork. On a globe or map, locate countries where these languages are spoken.

3. Big Book—Divide the class into 12 small groups. Each group takes one numerical phrase from the carol—for example, "Two turtledoves" or "Eight maids a-milking," etc. Children illustrate their phrases on pieces of poster board. Encourage them to decorate the borders as well. Sing or retell the story while displaying the appropriate page for each verse. The members of each group should stand behind their poster board illustration. Compile the pages into a big book and bind them sequentially under a cover created by the entire class. Place the big book in the reading corner with a cassette tape of the story.

Math

1. Counting—Practice counting objects with young children as you read each page. For example, count the seven swans, eight maids, etc.

2. Addition—Add the total number of objects in the story:

   1 partridge
   2 turtledoves
   3 French hens
   4 colly birds
   5 golden rings
   6 geese a-laying
   7 swans a-swimming
   8 maids a-milking
   9 drummers drumming
   10 pipers piping
   11 ladies dancing
   12 lords a-leaping
   78 total

Refer to the activity sheets on pages 35–36 for additional math practice. Activity sheets can be reprogrammed for counting practice by simply eliminating the total tally area.

The Twelve Days of Christmas (cont.)

Art

1. Popcorn and Cranberry Garlands—The family in the border artwork made popcorn garlands to decorate their tree. Encourage children to develop their fine motor skills by stringing popcorn and cranberries (be sure to use blunt-end needles). Hang the garlands for decoration inside the classroom or from trees outside for birds and squirrels to eat.

2. Decorate a Christmas Tree—Put up a Christmas tree in your classroom. Ask children to create ornaments for the tree.

3. Red and Green Paper Chains—Cut 1 1/2" (3.75 cm) wide strips of red and green construction paper. Have children form circles from the strips and interlock the circles to create a chain. Challenge children to create and follow a pattern—for example, red, green, red, green . . . or green, green, red, green, green, red . . . etc.

4. Snowball Soaps—Have students mix approximately 1/3 cup (83 mL) Ivory Snow laundry soap with a little water. Add laundry soap or water as necessary until mixture resembles mashed potatoes. Form into a ball and stick a sprig of plastic holly into the top of each snowball. Soap can be placed inside a paper muffin cup with a Christmas design on it. When completely dry, soaps can be wrapped to be given to parents as a gift.

5. Simmering Potpourri—Children gather the following items into a fabric bag which has been decorated with rubber stamps:

2 tablespoons (30 mL) whole cloves	3 cinnamon sticks
2 bay leaves	1 slice orange peel
1 slice lemon peel	1 small candy cane

This activity can be set out at a center with rebus directions for amounts to be placed inside the bag. Duplicate the following directions to place inside each bag:

Add 1 1/2 cups (375 mL) of water and bring to a boil. Reduce heat and simmer.

Music

1. "Feliz Navidad"—Introduce children to this song while learning to say "Merry Christmas" in different languages. Translate the Spanish words for your youngsters.

2. Sing Christmas songs in different languages—for example, "Stille Nacht" in German, "Adeste Fidelis" in Latin, "We Wish You a Merry Christmas" in sign language, etc.

3. Sing "The Twelve Days of Christmas."

4. Bagpipe Demonstration—Invite a bagpiper into the classroom to demonstrate how to play this Scottish instrument highlighted in the story.

Movement

1. Scottish Highland Dancing—Invite a group of dancers to demonstrate traditional Highland dances like the Flora MacDonald, Highland Fling, Seann Triuhas, Broadsword, etc. Teach children a simple dance like the Highland Fling.

2. "The Twelve Days of Christmas"—Act out the motions to the song while singing it with the children. See directions on page 37.

The Twelve Days of Christmas *(cont.)*

Cooking

My mother began a tradition by baking Christmas cookies and making candy with her children. Today, I carry on the tradition by making gingerbread cookies with my class. This is our award-winning family recipe. I hope you enjoy it! Did you notice the family in the border artwork baking gingerbread cookies?

Gingerbread Cookies

3 cups (750 mL) sifted flour

1 1/2 teaspoons (7 mL) baking powder

1/4 teaspoon (1 mL) salt

1/2 teaspoon (2 mL) baking soda

1/2 teaspoon (2mL) ginger

1 1/2 teaspoon (7 mL) cinnamon

1/2 cup (125 mL) melted margarine

1 cup (250 mL) molasses

2 tablespoons (30 mL) warm water

1 beaten egg

Sift dry ingredients together. Combine remaining ingredients and mix thoroughly. Let mixture stand about 10 minutes. Roll out on floured surface. Cut out cookies with gingerbread boy, girl and/or family cookie cutters and bake at 350° F (180° C) for 10 minutes.

Yield: 2 dozen

Confetti Candy Ice Cream

(Ingredients for classs of 24)

24 small candy canes

1 1/2 cups (375 mL) sugar

24 drops red food coloring

24 drops green food coloring

24 scoops ice cream

Break candy canes into small pieces by hand and place in resealable plastic bags. With a rolling pin, crush the small pieces into finer parts. Be careful not to break the bags. Place half the sugar in one bowl and add red food coloring. Place the remaining sugar in another bowl and add the green coloring. (More coloring may be added to each bowl if desired.) Sprinkle each scoop of ice cream with decorative candy cane bits and colored sugars.

The Twelve Days of Christmas

Addition Practice

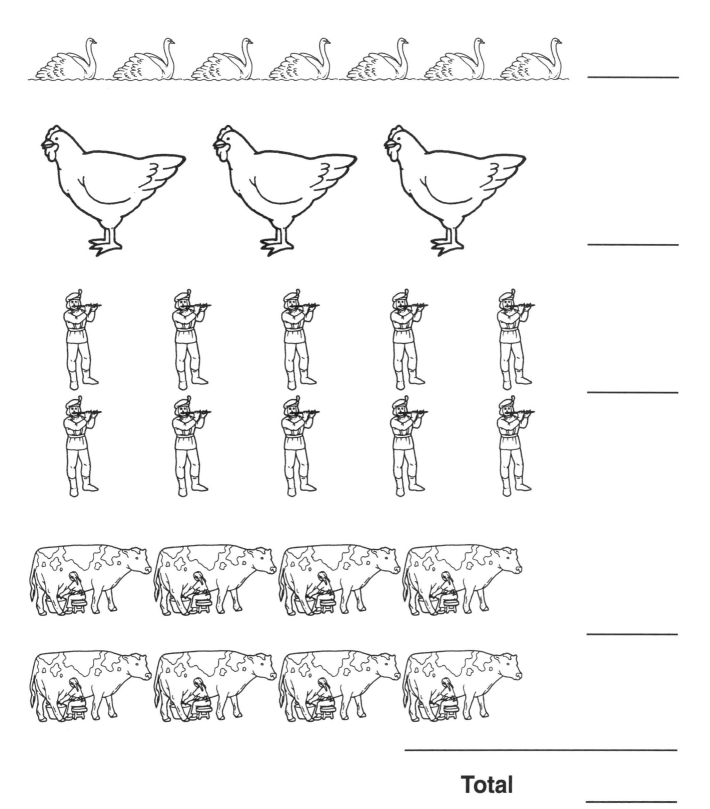

Total

© 1995 Teacher Created Materials, Inc.   35   # 454 Favorite Authors: Jan Brett

The Twelve Days of Christmas

Addition Practice (cont.)

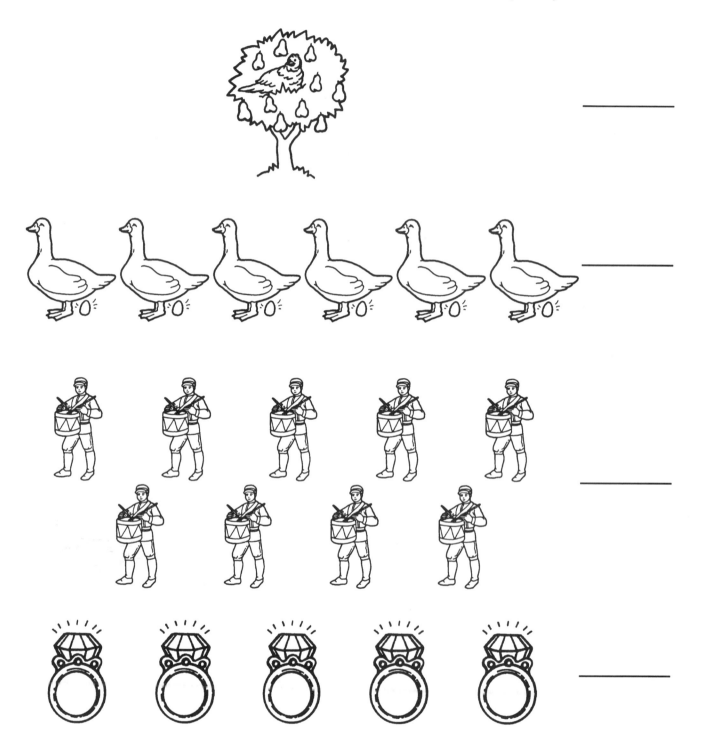

Total

The Twelve Days Of Christmas

Movement Activity Directions

A partridge—Turn to the right, stand on right foot; left foot bent and out behind you; right arm in air and left arm out at waist level.

In a pear tree—Stand on both feet, both arms overhead forming tree top.

Two turtledoves—Interlock the thumbs of each hand and move fingers together and apart twice. (Only fingertips should be touching; it will look like a butterfly flitting around.)

Three French hens—Place thumbs under your armpits and flap your arms.

Four colly birds—Cup hands around your mouth and yell "Four!" right after singing "birds."

Five gold rings—Form a circle with your right thumb and index finger; slide this "ring" over the fourth finger of your left hand.

Six geese a-laying—Place thumbs under armpits; squat down as if laying an egg.

Seven swans a-swimming—Stroke arms in forward "Australian crawl" position (or dog paddle rapidly).

Eight maids a-milking—Pull imaginary udders as if milking a cow.

Nine drummers drumming—Pretend to play drums with imaginary drumsticks.

Ten pipers piping—Pretend to play the bagpipes.

Eleven ladies dancing—Put left arm at waist and right arm in the air; twirl around once in place.

Twelve lords a-leaping—Leap into air and land in place.

© 1995 Teacher Created Materials, Inc.   37   #454 Favorite Authors: Jan Brett

The Wild Christmas Reindeer

Jan Brett was having some trouble with her horse, Westminster, about the time she decided to write a book about the North Pole. She noticed that when she was angry with him and lost her temper, he tended to be stubborn, and things just got worse. But when Brett took a deep breath and spoke calmly to Westminster, he was much more likely to listen and comply. With a change of setting and characters, Jan Brett converted her own real-life experiences into the story of a reindeer handler named Teeka.

Brett's model for Teeka was a girl named Natalie. Natalie acted out all of the parts of the story while Brett sketched and photographed her. Brett altered her story to better fit Natalie's personality by changing Teeka from an impatient and angry elf to a more thoughtful and determined one.

To prepare for the artwork, Jan Brett traveled to Norway where an 800-year-old stave church inspired her design of the reindeer barn. She visited folk museums where she saw beautiful designs on sleighs, clocks, spoons, harnesses, and blankets.

Her research led her to the University of Maine where she photographed some very affectionate caribou. The reindeer in Jan Brett's book are the great-great-grandchildren of the caribou immortalized in the famous story *Rudolph the Red-Nosed Reindeer*. Each of the reindeer has a distinct personality. Tundra is the noble leader who likes to be first. Snowball is pure white, chubby, and always hungry. Crag is the grumpy loner. The dark, mysterious reindeer is Twilight. Heather, who is easily frightened, has big brown eyes. The aptly named Bramble has twisted antlers, while Windswept is easily carried away. The eighth reindeer, Lichen, has mossy-looking markings on his coat.

The first date that appears in the book's borders is December 1. That is not only an appropriate starting point for a Christmas book; it is also Jan Brett's birthday. *The Wild Christmas Reindeer* was on *The New York Times* bestseller list.

Language Arts

1. Read *The Wild Christmas Reindeer*. Discuss Teeka's methods for training the reindeer. Which worked best? Why?

   How did Teeka feel about the special job Santa gave her?

   What mistakes did she make with the reindeer?

   What made Teeka realize she was doing the wrong thing?

   What lesson did Teeka learn?

2. Predicting—Display the cover of the book prior to reading the story. Ask children to describe what is happening.

   Tell them that Santa has given Teeka an important job.

   Encourage the children to predict what her job could be.

   Write predictions on chart paper with the child's name or initials next to them. Read the story. Review the predictions. Compare and contrast them to what actually happens in *The Wild Christmas Reindeer*.

The Wild Christmas Reindeer *(cont.)*

Language Arts *(cont.)*

3. Fingerplay

  A. Santa Claus

   Here is the chimney,

   Here is the top,

   Open the lid,

   And out Santa will pop!

  B. When Santa Comes

   When Santa comes to our house,

   I would like to peek,

   But I know he'll never come,

   Until I'm fast asleep!

4. Writing Letters—Encourage the children to write to Santa, Teeka, a reindeer, or an elf. They can tell Santa what they would like for Christmas, ask Teeka questions about being a reindeer-handler, or ask the elves all about Santa's Winterfarm Workshop and what is behind the tower gates. Display a sample letter on chart paper. Explain that each letter has a salutation (greeting), body, closing, and signature. Ask the children to imitate the proper letter-writing format and encourage them to illustrate the margins (or borders) of their letters.

5. Adjective Word Bank—Create a word bank describing the reindeer in the story—e.g., gentle, soft, chubby, grumpy, friendly, affectionate, etc. Do the same for their feelings during the story—e,g., bewildered, confused, frightened, upset, angry, sad, etc.

Math/Science

1. Favorite Project Graph—Show border illustrations to the students. Point out the different projects that the elves are finishing. Ask each child to vote for his/her favorite elf project.

2. Toy/Baker Elf Classification—Have children sort pictures of toys and Christmas goodies into correct categories. Copy, color, and laminate the pictures on pages 42-43 for this activity.

3. Caribou Facts—Show pictures of real caribou to the children. Bring a World Wildlife Foundation stuffed caribou to show the class. Discuss and share the following facts on caribou with the class.

   - Caribou are commonly named *reindeer.*
   - Caribou fur is thick.
   - Caribou males and females both grow antlers.
   - Caribou antlers are bone; they feel soft like velvet.
   - Caribou antlers fall off each year in the late fall.
   - Caribou mothers usually have one baby in the spring.
   - Caribou eat moss, grass, twigs, bark, shrubs, etc.
   - Caribou run 40–50 mph.
   - Caribou enemies are wolves and bears.

The Wild Christmas Reindeer (cont.)

Math/Science (cont.)

4. Calendar—Have children fill in each dated space on the December calendar with a toy picture as a countdown to Christmas. Reproduce the calendar on page 44 for each child.
5. Machines and Toys—After discussing the toys being built in the borders by the elves, introduce the children to simple machines (magnets, inclined plane, pulleys, batteries, etc.) and how they work.
6. Topography—Discuss tundra. Show children real moss. Talk about other types of topography— e.g., desert, rain forest, swamp, etc.

Art

1. Lunch Sack Reindeer—Trace and cut yellow construction paper handprints (antlers). Glue on antlers, red or brown pompon nose, and wiggly eyes. Stuff sack with newspaper and tie shut at the top.
2. Reindeer Headbands—Have children cut out brown antlers. Use red or brown face paint on their noses.
3. Favorite Elf Project—Assist students as they create a simplified version of the most popular project (see math activity #1). Photograph the students at work and display the pictures in a pretty tower cutout similar to a tower in the book's borders.
4. Antlers Painting—Encourage the children to paint at the easels with reindeer antlers (tree branches). When the painting dries, it can be used to wrap Christmas presents to parents.

Music

1. Play "Rudolph the Red-Nosed Reindeer" on *Raffi's Christmas Album*.
2. Play "Up on the Housetop" on *Raffi's Christmas Album*.
3. Play "Must Be Santa" on *Raffi's Christmas Album*.

Movement

"Reindeer Pokey"
(tune: Hokey Pokey)
You put your antlers in,
You put your antlers out,
You put your antlers in,
And you poke them all about,
You do the Reindeer Pokey,
And you prance yourself around,
That's what it's all about!

(Verse 2: You put your tail in and you swish it all about . . .)
(Verse 3: You put your front legs in and you paw them all about . . .)
(Verse 4: You put your hind legs in and you stamp them all about . . .)
(Verse 5: You put your whole body in and you prance it all about . . .)

The Wild Christmas Reindeer *(cont.)*

Cooking

Reindeer Treats

Spread half a graham cracker with peanut butter. Add two pretzel antlers, two raisin eyes and a red or brown m & m's nose. Write out rebus directions for children to follow to construct their own snacks.

Reindeer Food—See note to parents on page 45.

Reindeer Gingerplum Cake

1 package gingerbread mix

1 cup (250 mL) canned plums (chopped)

1/2 teaspoon (2 mL) salt

3/4 cup (185 mL) chopped walnuts

1 cup (250 mL) raisins

1 can prepared whipped cream

1 jar of canned cherry halves

Prepare gingerbread mixture in a large bowl and add chopped plums, salt, chopped nuts, and raisins. (You may substitute remaining plum juice for half the liquid called for in the package mix.)

Pour the mixture into a greased and floured angel food cake pan. Bake at 375° F (190° C) for 50–55 minutes (or until an inserted toothpick comes out clean). Let cool for 30 minutes. Slice sections and decorate with whipped cream and canned cherry halves to make wild (Rudolph) reindeer faces.

Life Skill—Cooperation

1. Play cooperation games with the children—for example, Squirrels in Trees, London Bridge, etc.

2. Pair children together for a day. They are to help each other with work and are buddies during free play.

3. Evaluate at the end of the day and relate these activities to how the reindeer in the story cooperated or learned to work together.

The Wild Christmas Reindeer

Toy/Baker Elf Classification

#454 Favorite Authors: Jan Brett   42   © 1995 Teacher Created Materials, Inc.

The Wild Christmas Reindeer

Toy/Baker Elf Classification (cont.)

The Wild Christmas Reindeer

Calendar

Note: Program calendar dates prior to copying.

The Wild Christmas Reindeer

Reindeer Food

Reindeer Food

We will be mixing a treat for Santa's reindeer. Please send 2 cups of the following with your child on: _____

- Cheerios • Raisins • Nuts
- Sunflower seeds
- Pretzels • m&m's
- Chocolate chips

Your Child will bring home a bag of reindeer food to put out on Christmas Eve. We hope all the little reindeer enjoy it !! Ho-Ho-Ho

The Mitten

Three teachers who were good friends mentioned to Jan Brett at a book signing that she should adapt and illustrate the Ukrainian folktale *The Mitten*. Before Brett began working, a Ukrainian woman named Oxana Piaseckyj translated different versions of the story into English for her. At the Ukrainian Museum in New York City, Brett learned that many children in the Ukraine wear hand-me-downs, so she decided to outfit the child in the story with oversized clothes. She also learned that it is a Ukrainian custom to hang a water jug on a fence so that passersby can get a drink and that among Ukrainians a stork's nest on a cottage roof is believed to bring good luck. *The Mitten* is dedicated to the three teachers who originally suggested the idea to Brett. Tad Beagley, the fourth person to whom the book is dedicated, was the model for Nicki and, of course, the mouse is Little Pearl! Brett photographed Tad as he climbed trees, jumped walls, and leaped in the air. She chose him because he was full of energy like Nicki. Brett's mother, Jean, was the model for Baba. She changed her hair from shiny brown to snowy white and added a long braid.

Jan Brett visited a wildlife refuge in England named St. Tiggywinkles so she could draw a hedgehog, her favorite animal. Hedgehogs are gentle, determined creatures. They are the size of guinea pigs and curl up in a ball to protect themselves from predators. Their natural instinct is to turn objects over while looking for destructive insects to eat. *The Mitten* is one of *Booklist's* Best Books for the 80s.

Language Arts

1. Read *The Mitten*. Help students locate Ukraine on the globe or a map. Explain the significance of the jug and the stork's nest to the children. Re-examine the book to look for these details.

2. Recall/Memory Skills—Read the story. Stop after a number of the animals are inside the mitten and ask the children to list them.

3. Retelling the Story—Allow children to retell the tale using a felt mitten and stuffed-felt characters from the story. Use the patterns on pages 49–51 (or have children make craft-stick puppets from these patterns).

4. "Three Little Kittens Rhyme"—Share this favorite nursery rhyme with the class. Ask children if they have ever lost their mittens (or some similar piece of clothing) and then found them in some unexpected place. Have children write stories about losing the items and where they finally discovered them.

5. Language Enrichment—Explain vocabulary words as necessary—e.g., *mole, hedgehog, badger, silhouetted, enormous, lumbered, plumped, waft, drowsy, commotion, swooped, glinty, talons, snuffling, jostled, admire*, etc.

6. Mitten Books—Have the children cut two white and two colored mitten shapes from construction paper. Staple the white sheets between the colored ones to make a booklet. Challenge the children to think of some unusual contents for a mitten. Have children illustrate and label their ideas. Provide art supplies to decorate the colored, mitten-shaped covers of their booklet.

The Mitten (cont.)

Language Arts (cont.)

7. Bloom's Taxonomy of Higher Order Questions:

   Knowledge—Describe how the mitten changed throughout the story.

   Which animal was the first to enter the mitten?

   Comprehension—Why did the mitten explode?

   Explain all of the reasons the animals allowed the others to come into the mitten.

   Application—If you had to ask one animal to leave, which one would it be and why?

   If your grandmother wanted to make you a pair of mittens, which color would you request and why?

   Analysis—How does Jan Brett's version of the story differ from Alvin Tresselt's?

   Examine all of the reasons a mitten might be a good house or a bad house for a mole.

   Synthesis—How would the story be different if the bear did not sneeze?

   Design a new house for the animals that would comfortably accommodate them all.

   Evaluation—Which version of *The Mitten* do you like better? Why? Judge which character might be the best roommate for the mole and explain your reasons.

8. Writing Invitations—Write an invitation from Nicki to the other animals, inviting them to his mitten.

Math/Science

1. Size Seriation—As the cast of characters is introduced one by one, children will no doubt notice that each animal is a bit bigger than the preceding one (except for the mouse). Clip animal pictures (which are to scale) from magazines. Mount onto tagboard and laminate. To create a storage pocket for the cards, cut two tagboard mittens. Punch holes around the mittens and stitch them together. To use the activity, a child lines up the pictures in order from smallest to largest.

2. Mitten/Glove Graph—Graph the children's actual mittens/gloves. Ask children open-ended questions like "What do you notice about our graph?" or "Do you think anything should be placed in a different spot?"

3. Mitten Match/Pairs—Have children pair the mittens (use the children's real ones, if possible). As they work, ask them to describe what they are searching for—for example, "I'm looking for one that has a pink heart," etc.

4. Mitten and Interlocking Cubes—Pretend that the interlocking cubes are animals. Have the children fill their mittens with interlocking cubes. Then have them count the number of cubes inside their mittens. Ask each child to arrange cubes by color (sorting) and then to seriate rows by quantity. Ask each child to tell which color he/she used most, least, or whether there were any used in equal quantities. Children can form small groups, combine their cubes, and repeat the process.

© 1995 Teacher Created Materials, Inc. 47 # 454 Favorite Authors: Jan Brett

The Mitten (cont.)

Art

1. **Mittens**—Prepare mitten-shaped pairs cut from 5" x 8" (12.5 cm. x 20 cm) pastel index cards. Knot a yarn length in the first hole. Have children stitch and decorate the mittens.

   Bulletin Board Display—Hang mittens from a clothesline. Arrange felt animals around them and write the "Three Little Kittens" rhyme above them.

Music

"The Mitten Song"
(tune: "Skip to My Lou")
Thumbs in the thumb place, fingers all together,
This is the song we sing in mitten weather,
Doesn't matter whether, they're made of wool or leather,
Thumbs in the thumb place, fingers all together.

Drama

Circle Story Drama—Dramatize the story while sitting in a circle formation. Double and triple-cast characters so that every child has a part to perform. Use a parachute stretched over the circle to represent the mitten. Ask children who are unwilling to perform parts to hold the parachute. When the mitten explodes, these children stand up, twirl around once and sit down on the circle. The "animals" inside the parachute roll on the floor in all directions. The teacher should perform the lead (the mole) with one or two children. Try to encourage the children to ad-lib lines rather than speaking lines verbatim.

Games

Mitten, Mitten, Who Has the Mitten?—Children sit in a circle. Ask them to recall the animals from *The Mitten*. Assign each child an animal from the story. The teacher portrays Nicki. Pretend to gather firewood. Walk in front of a child and accidentally drop the mitten. Ask, "Mitten, mitten, who has the mitten?" Instead of the child answering "I do," she/he must answer with the animal name, "The rabbit has your mitten." The child who has the mitten becomes the next Nicki.

Pat-a-Cake—Play pat-a-cake, using a variation of The Doctor-Nurse-Lady verses and substituting "mittens" for "the measles," etc.

"Mittens," said the doctor,
"Gloves," said the nurse,
"Earmuffs," said the lady
With the alligator purse.

"Freezing," said the doctor,
"Cold," said the nurse,
"Chilly," said the lady
With the alligator purse.

"Stay warm," said the doctor,
"Bundle," said the nurse,
"Brrrr!" said the lady
With the alligator purse.

The Mitten

Mitten Story Animal Patterns

Directions

To make felt animals, cut two of each and stitch together. Leave a seam opening large enough to stuff. Stuff with cotton and sew the seam shut.

© 1995 Teacher Created Materials, Inc. #454 Favorite Authors: Jan Brett

The Mitten

Mitten Story Animal Patterns *(cont.)*

Note: Enlarge mitten to 15" x 12" (38 cm x 30 cm). Do not stuff. Sew along seam, except for one edge. Attach Velcro to the unstitched edge for use when the mitten bursts open.

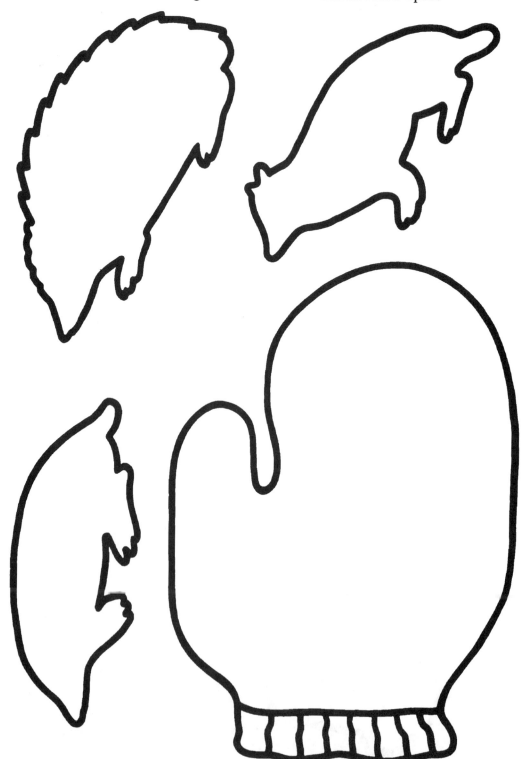

#454 Favorite Authors: Jan Brett © 1995 Teacher Created Materials, Inc.

The Mitten

Mitten Story Animal Patterns *(cont.)*

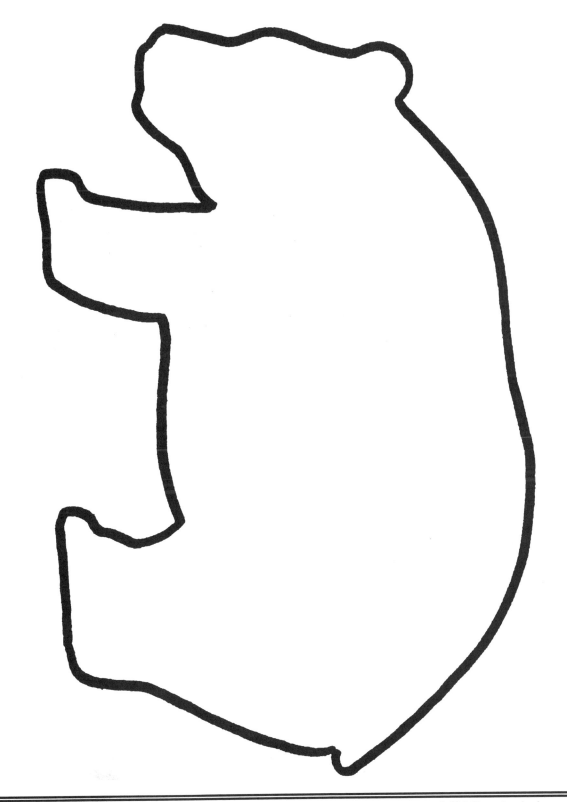

Annie and the Wild Animals

If you are studying the seasons, *Annie and the Wild Animals* is an excellent read-aloud choice. In this story, Annie's cat becomes unusually antisocial and wanders off into the wilderness, leaving Annie lonely. Observant readers can scan the detailed borders to find out what is happening in the woods around Annie as she tries to lure another animal for a pet.

Language Arts

1. Read *Annie and the Wild Animals.* Allow children an opportunity to discuss their pets and the special bonds they have with them.

2. Setting—Ask children to describe the setting in the first half of *Annie and the Wild Animals* and compare it to the second half. Encourage students to describe the changes they see occurring in the illustrations.

Math/Science

1. Seasons—After reading the book aloud, have children closely examine the pictures in the first half of the book. Ask them to describe the setting. Then have children describe the changes in the setting as they examine the second half of the book. Ask students to name each season represented in the book.

2. Winter Patterns—Have children complete the pattern of winter clothes on the activity sheet on page 55.

3. Calendar—Have students mark how many days Annie fed the animals. Then have them count the number of days and then count how many days it is until spring.

4. Kittens—Invite children with kittens to share them with the class. Discuss how to properly care for a pet.

5. Weather Chart—Copy the weather chart on page 56 for each child. Have them mark off the type of weather occurring daily for one month. At the end of the month, they should count and tabulate the total number of sunny, partly cloudy, cloudy, rainy, snowy, and foggy days. Compare results in small groups.

6. Temperature Changes—Fill the texture table 1/4 of the way full with tap water. Place a thermometer into the water and record the temperature on the activity sheet provided (page 57). Dump a bucket full of snow into the texture table. Record the temperature 10 minutes later, 30 minutes later and one hour later. Ask children to explain the temperature fluctuations.

7. Melting Race—Have each child collect a small cupful of snow and put it somewhere in the classroom. Check the snow every 5–10 minutes. With the children, keep a chart with these headings:

   Name, Location of Cup, and **Order of Melting**

   Ask children to explain why snow in certain locations melted faster/slower than others.

Note: Ice cubes can be substituted for snow in activities #6 and #7 if you live in an area where it does not snow.

8. Snowflake Observation—Place large sheets of dark construction paper in the freezer. Later, catch snowflakes on the paper and look at them with magnifying lenses.

 # 454 Favorite Authors: Jan Brett   *© 1995 Teacher Created Materials, Inc.*

Annie and the Wild Animals *(cont.)*

Math/Science *(cont.)*

9. Winter Clothes Classification—Have students sort pictures of clothes into winter and summer categories. Use pictures on pages 58–59 for this activity. Simply copy, color, and laminate for durability.

10. Frost Experiment—Have students mix two cups (500 mL) of crushed ice with 1/2 cup (125 mL) rock salt in a one-pound coffee can. Wait 30 minutes. Observe the outside of the can. (It will have dew on it. Wait a little longer, and the dew will turn to frost.)

11. Snowball Toss—Direct students to throw 2" – 3" (5cm – 7.5 cm) diameter Styrofoam balls into bucket #1, #2, or #3. You can teach ordinal numbers by starting the direction in the following manner: "Throw the ball into the second bucket." This activity makes an excellent excusing game.

12. Pine Cone Study—Ask students to tell you everything they know about pine trees. Point out the pine trees in Jan Brett's pictures. Discuss the fact that pine cones are the seeds produced by pine trees. Have each child select five pine cones. Ask them to arrange pinecones by size (seriation). Have them estimate the number of scales on one of their pine cones. Ask them to pull the scales off and count them. Compare the numbers to their estimates.

Art

1. Four Seasons—Each student paints a toilet paper tube brown to represent a tree trunk. Cut two small paper plates in half and cut slits in top of the toilet paper tube for the plates to slip into. Decorate each half-plate to represent each season. Some suggestions follow:

    Fall—Paint one half-plate green. Then paint brown branches and glue green, orange, red and yellow tissue paper leaves to the treetop.

    Winter—Paint brown branches and attach white cottonball snow.

    Spring—Paint brown branches and glue green tissue paper buds to tree branches.

    Summer—Glue green tissue paper onto plate and red tissue-paper apples (crumpled into balls).

2. Pussy Willows—Draw brown branches on white construction paper. Glue on Puffed Rice cereal.

3. Daffodils—Students tint a coffee filter yellow with food coloring. Attach a yellow baking cup to the center. Mount on the bulletin board. Allow children to attach stems and leaves they have cut from green construction paper. Post the following verse on the bulletin board with the daffodils:

    A little yellow cup,

    A little yellow frill,

    A star in the middle,

    And that's a daffodil!

Annie and the Wild Animals (cont.)

Art (cont.)

4. Pine Cone Painting—Place easel paper into a box lid. Have students dip a pine cone into paint and roll it around inside the box lid. When dry, the paper can be cut into notecards and given as a gift to a parent or a grandparent.

5. Snowy Pine Trees (large group project)—Cut a large pine tree out of green construction paper. Have students use white shoe polish applicators to add snow effect. Glue on white cotton if you desire more snow.

Cooking

Corn Muffins

1 cup (250 mL) cornmeal

1 cup (250 mL) sifted flour

1 teaspoon (5 mL) salt

2 tablespoons (30 mL) sugar

4 teaspoons (20 mL) baking powder

1 egg

1 cup (250 mL) milk

2 tablespoons (30 mL) butter or margarine

Sift dry ingredients together. Beat egg and add milk and butter. Add dry ingredients and mix only until blended. Fill muffin cups 2/3 full and bake at 350° F (180° C) for 30–35 minutes.

Yield: 12 muffins

Pine Cone Treats

3 ounces (90 g) softened cream cheese

1/2 cup (125 mL) shredded cheddar cheese

1 tablespoon (15 mL) frozen apple juice concentrate

1 cup (250 mL) grated carrots

1/2 cup (125 mL) chopped walnuts

Cream together cream cheese, cheddar cheese and concentrate. Stir in carrots and form mixture into balls. Roll in walnuts.

Yield: 8–10 large balls

Life Skill—Friendship

Role-play situations involving the establishment and maintenance of friendships.

Annie and the Wild Animals

Winter Patterns

Directions: Cut out the pictures at the bottom of the page. Glue a picture in the space provided to finish the pattern.

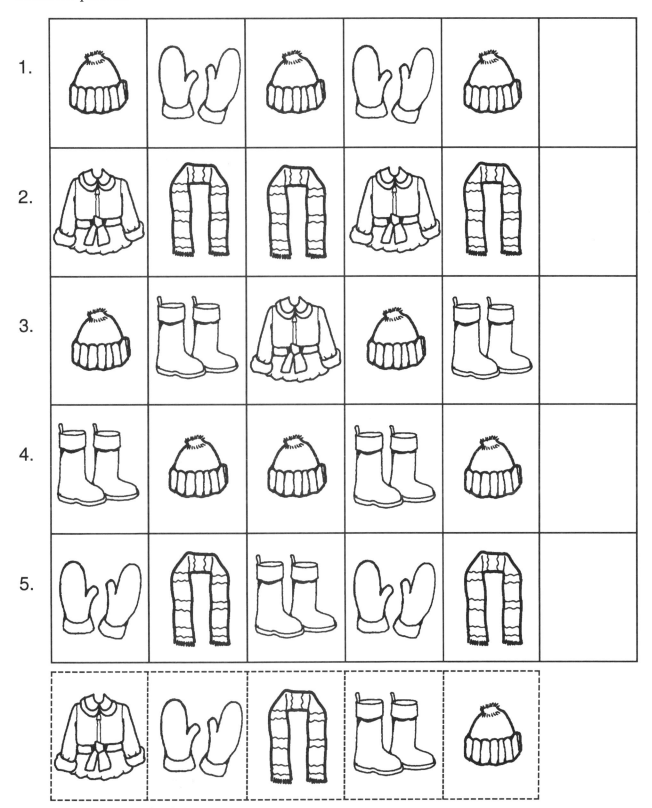

© 1995 Teacher Created Materials, Inc. 55 # 454 Favorite Authors: Jan Brett

Annie and the Wild Animals

Weather Graph

Directions: Color in one weather box each day. At the end of a month, count the number of days for each type of weather.

Use this row for a local weather symbol.

Temperature Changes

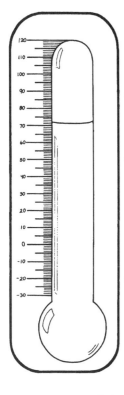

Time _____

Conditions

_____

_____

Temperature _____

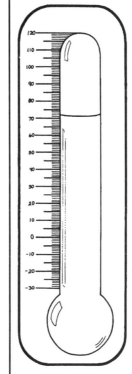

Time _____

Conditions

_____

_____

Temperature _____

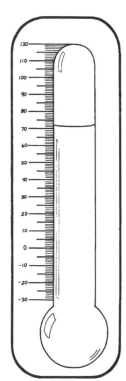

Time _____

Conditions

_____

_____

Temperature _____

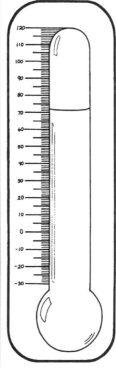

Time _____

Conditions

_____

_____

Temperature _____

Annie and the Wild Animals

Summer Clothes Classification

Annie and the Wild Animals

Winter Clothes Classification

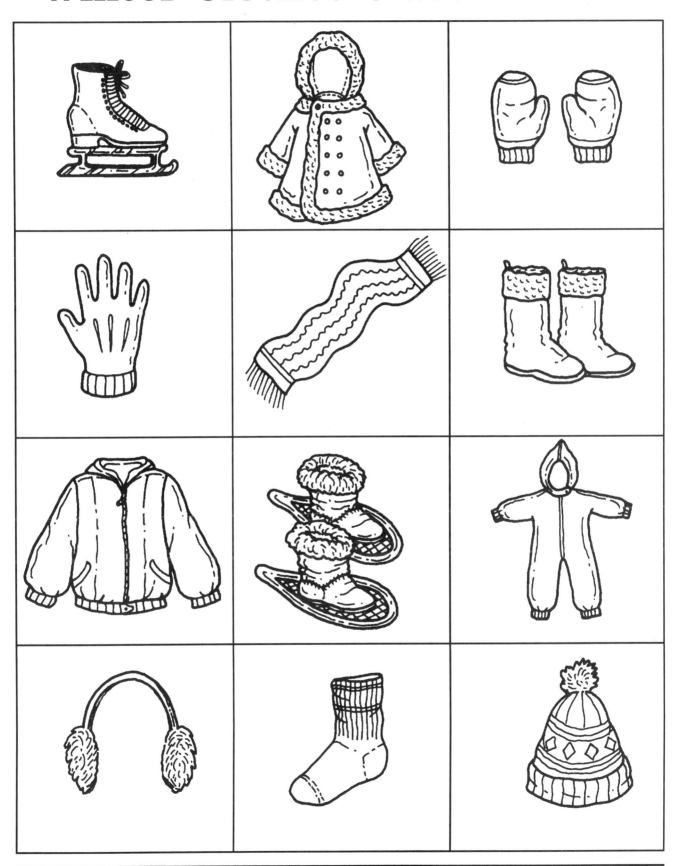

The First Dog

Perky Pumpkin is the name of Jan Brett's Siberian husky. After marveling at all the different expressions her dog made, she came up with the idea of putting Perky Pumpkin in a story. Part of Brett's inspiration for *The First Dog* came from her visits to the American Museum of Natural History's exhibit "Dark Caves, Bright Visions: Life in Ice Age Europe" and from the George C. Page Museum of La Brea Discoveries where she found on display a saber-tooth cat skull with its sabers still intact. After viewing these Ice Age artifacts and cave drawings, Jan Brett wrote and illustrated *The First Dog,* a Reading Rainbow book.

Language Arts

1. Read *The First Dog.* Explain to your students that this story is Jan Brett's idea of how the first relationship between a person and a dog developed. Have children look closely at the pictures of Paleowolf again, asking them to describe each of his expressions. Ask them if they have ever noticed similar looks on their own pets and what they think those expressions might mean. Pick out some pictures of Paleowolf exhibiting different expressions (enlarge them with an opaque projector if necessary). Ask the students what they think he might have said if he had been able to talk. Write their responses on Post-it notes stuck on the page somewhere near Paleowolf. Read *The First Dog* again, inserting the wolf's comments where appropriate.

2. Bloom's Taxonomy of Higher Order Questions:

    Knowledge—What was Kip eating?

    Comprehension—Why was Paleowolf following Kip?

    Application—If you were Kip, what would you have taken with you to protect yourself from enemies?

    Analysis—Compare Paleowolf to a dog. How are they alike? How are they different?

    Synthesis—How would the story have changed if Paleowolf had not warned Kip about the danger?

    Evaluation—Do you wish you could have lived during the Ice Age? Why or why not?

3. Adjective Word Bank—Collect words while reading through *The First Dog* to add to your class adjective word bank—e.g., *keen, fine, sharp, wrinkled, narrowed, resounded, roasted, toasted, crispy, crunchy, pearly, greasy, glowed, shimmer, sparkle,* etc.

 # 454 Favorite Authors: Jan Brett   *© 1995 Teacher Created Materials, Inc.*

The First Dog (cont.)

Math/Science

1. **Prehistoric Sets**—Have students use dinosaurs to make sets as directed. Copy, color, and laminate the dinosaurs on pages 65–67.

    Here's a group of reptiles,
    But they are not the same;
    Let's make some sets of dinosaurs,
    And group them all by name.

    Here is Tyrannosaurus Rex,
    They say he weighed eight tons;
    He's in a set all by itself,
    'Cause he's the only one!

    Here we see Pteranodon,
    He flies in skies so blue;
    Find the dinosaur with wings,
    And make a set of two.

    Here we see Triceratops,
    He has three horns, you see;
    Find all the dinosaurs with frills,
    And make a set of three.

    Here we see Elasmosaurus
    Now can you find some more?
    Look for dinosaurs that swim,
    And make a set of four.

The poem may be recorded and set at a listening center for children to perform the actions independently.

2. **Where Do They Belong?** (classification—land, sea, air)

    Have students sort dinosaurs into appropriate habitats. This activity can be placed on a bulletin board if you use large visuals (available at most teacher supply stores). The activity sheets on pages 68–70 can be used with dinosaur models or the small dinosaur cutouts on page 71.

3. **Dinosaur Fossil Observation**—Explain that scientists (paleontologists) know what dinosaurs looked like because they have fossils of dinosaur skeletons. Place magnifying lenses and real fossils from the age of dinosaurs on the science table for children to explore during free play. (These are available from many school science supply houses.)

4. **Information About Dinosaurs**—An excellent source for information on dinosaurs is the Wildlife Education series of *Zoobooks* (which includes two volumes on dinosaurs). See pages 65-67 for condensed fact-sheets on dinosaurs.

© 1995 Teacher Created Materials, Inc.   61   # 454 Favorite Authors: Jan Brett

The First Dog (cont.)

Art

1. Cave Drawings Mural—Spray a length of white bulletin board paper with gray or faux granite paint. When the paint has dried, cut the paper in the shape of a boulder and attach it to a bulletin board. After studying the illustrations in the borders of *The First Dog*, have each student use chalk, markers, crayons, etc., to draw on the boulder what she/he would have drawn on a cave wall if she/he had lived during the Ice Age.

2. Salt Dough Dog Tag Necklaces—Students create a dog tag similar to Paleowolf's from salt dough. Punch a hole in the dough and tint the dough with food coloring prior to baking it (the child can use an eye dropper to do this). After the tags have cooled from baking, attach a leather shoestring to each tag's hole.

   Salt Dough

   2 parts flour

   1 part salt

   Add just enough water to make a dough. Form into desired shape. Food coloring can be dropped onto dough before baking. Bake at 300° F (150° C) for one hour (longer if the dough is thick).

3. Stegosaurus Hats—Cut open a grocery sack. Fold the sack lengthwise and trace three to four spikes. Have the students cut out spikes and sponge paint the entire sack (it will need to be opened). When dry, fold back one end as shown and staple. Students place this over their heads with the spikes hanging down their backs.

4. Fossilized Dinosaurs—Simulate fossilization by making plaster of Paris "fossils." Pour plaster into a Styrofoam tray and allow it to harden slightly. Have students place objects—for example, hand, plastic dinosaur figurine, pine cone, wadded-up aluminum foil, kitchen utensils, etc., into the plaster. (DO NOT SUBMERGE ENTIRELY.)

Music

Learn the "Dinosaur Ditty" (song) in *The Best of the Mailbox,* Preschool/Kindergarten edition (See page 111.)

The First Dog (cont.)

Game

Dinosaur, Dinosaur, Where's Your Bone? The Paleontologist Came and Took It Home!—One child sits in the middle of the circle and covers her/his eyes. Place a "dinosaur" bone behind this child. Another child sneaks up and takes the bone. This child hides the bone behind his/her back. All the children place their hands behind their backs as if they are hiding the bone. Everyone recites the above rhyme. The original child receives three chances to guess the identity of the paleontologist.

Cooking

Puppy Chow

1 cup (250 mL) chocolate chips

1 1/2 cups (375 mL) peanut butter

1/4 cup (83 mL) margarine

8-9 cups (2 L) Rice Chex

1 box powdered sugar

Melt chocolate chips and peanut butter with margarine. Pour over Rice Chex in a large bowl. Put powdered sugar in large resealable plastic bag and pour the coated mixture into the bag. Shake until well coated with powdered sugar. Store in an airtight container.

Gingerbread Dog Bones

3 cups (750 mL) sifted flour

1 1/2 teaspoons (7.5 mL) baking powder

1/4 teaspoon (1 mL) salt

1/2 teaspoon (2 mL) ginger

1 1/2 teaspoons (7.5 mL) cinnamon

1/2 cup (125mL) melted margarine

1 cup (250 mL) molasses

2 tablespoons (30 mL) warm water

1 beaten egg

Sift dry ingredients together. Combine remaining ingredients and mix thoroughly. Let mixture stand about 10 minutes. Roll out on floured surface, cut out cookies with dog bone cookie cutters and bake at 350° F (180° C) for 10 minutes.

Yield: 2 1/2 dozen

© 1995 Teacher Created Materials, Inc.   #454 Favorite Authors: Jan Brett

The First Dog *(cont.)*

Cooking *(cont.)*

Dinosaur Eggs

3/4 cup (188 mL) honey
1 cup (250 mL) peanut butter
1 teaspoon (5 mL) cinnamon
1 1/2 (375 mL) cups powdered milk
1 cup (250 mL) wheat germ

Mix all ingredients together and form into egg shapes. Divide eggs in half and insert gummy dinosaurs. Remold egg shapes.

Yield: 25

Dog Treats

The following recipe can be made with the children. Dog treats can be donated to the Humane Society or a shelter in your area. They are NOT to be eaten by children.

3 1/2 cups (875 mL) unbleached flour
2 cups (500 mL) whole wheat flour
1 cup (250 mL) rye flour
2 cups (500 mL) cracked wheat
1 cup (250 mL) cornmeal
1/2 cup (125 mL) powdered milk
4 teaspoons (20 mL) salt
1 package active yeast
1/4 cup (63 mL) warm water
3 cups (750 mL) chicken broth

Mix flours, cracked wheat, cornmeal, powdered milk, and salt. Dissolve yeast in warm water and add to dry ingredients. Stir in chicken broth. Roll out dough to 1/4" (.63 cm) thick and cut with a dog-bone cookie cutter. Place on greased cookie sheet and bake 45 minutes at 300° F (150° C).

Dinosaur Delight

Give each child two pieces of hot dog, two broccoli florets and some salad dressing. Talk about the meat-eating dinosaurs as the children devour their hot dog pieces and the plant-eating dinosaurs as they munch their broccoli dipped in salad dressing. Point out that meat-eaters had lots of sharp teeth while plant-eaters had square, flat teeth.

Discovery Table—Sifting for Fossils

Place dry bleached chicken bones in a sand table. Allow children to use sieves to sift for dinosaurs. When they discover bones, have them brush them off with paint brushes and tag their discoveries.

Dinosaur Facts

Archeopteryx
(ar-kee-OP-ter-ix)

- "Ancient One With Wings"
- small primitive bird about 1 ½ feet (46 cm) long
- teeth like a reptile
- small wings with fingers
- climbed trees
- could not flap wings easily
- wingspan of 2 feet (61 cm)

Pteranodon
(tair-AN-o-don)

- looked like a bird
- large crest on the back of its head
- short body; large head
- small back legs
- short tail
- front legs attached to wings like a bat's
- wingspan of 20 feet (6 m)

Apatosaurus
(ah-PAT-uh-sawr-us)

- "Deceptive Lizard"
- common name—Brontosaurus or "Thundering Lizard"
- four legs like an elephant
- 75 feet (22.5 m) long; tail, 30 feet (9 m)
- giraffe-like neck
- ate plants
- ran 2-4 mph
- weighed 6 ½ pounds (2.9 kg) at birth

Dinosaur Facts (cont.)

Stegosaurus
(STEG-uh-sawr-us)

- "Roof Lizard"
- two rows of bony plates
- small head
- brain the size of a walnut
- four sharp spikes on tail
- about 20 feet (6 m) long

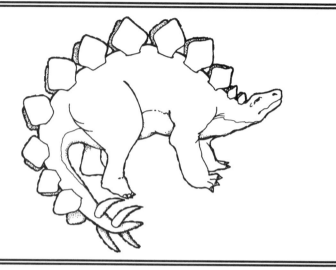

Triceratops
(try-SER-uh-tops)

- "Three Horns"
- three sharp horns and a hard bony collar
- looked like a rhinoceros
- ate plants
- smooth, round frill over shoulders
- hind legs longer than front legs
- short, heavy tail

Tyrannosaurus Rex
(tih-RAN-uh-sawr-us)

- "Tyrant Lizard"
- king of the dinosaurs
- largest meat-eating hunter
- 47 feet (14.1 m) long
- small front legs
- ran 40 mph
- powerful jaws
- strong legs and tail

Dinosaur Facts (cont.)

Ichthyosaurus
(IK-thi-uh-sawr-us)

- "Fish Lizard"
- swam in the seas
- long beak
- four paddlelike flippers
- tapering body resembling a dolphin
- tail with large fin

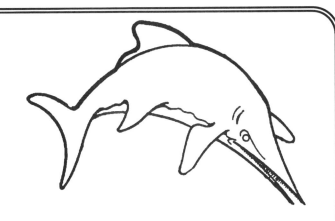

Ankylosaurus
(ang-KILE-uh-sawr-us)

- "Crooked (or curved) Lizard"
- armored body
- triangular-shaped head
- body about 6 feet (2 m) wide
- about 25 feet (7.5 m) long
- row of sharp spikes on sides and back
- thick, bony club at end of tail

Elasmosaurus
(e-LAS-muh-sawr-us)

- "Thin-plated Lizard"
- swam in warm oceans
- flippers shaped like paddles
- short tail and body
- long, thin neck

The First Dog

Where Do They Belong?

Land

Where Do They Belong? (cont.)

Water

The First Dog

Where Do They Belong? *(cont.)*

Air

The First Dog

Where Do They Belong? (cont.)
Dinosaur Cards

Directions: Copy, color, and laminate the cards below for use with this activity. Store them in a resealable bag.

The Owl and the Pussycat

To create the artwork for *The Owl and the Pussycat,* Jan Brett and her husband traveled to the Caribbean island of Martinique. There she found inspiration in the landscape and in the sea, which provides the setting for her unique interpretation of Edward Lear's classic poem. Brett chose "The Owl and the Pussycat" because it was her favorite poem as a child. Two items have always fascinated her about this poem—the *runcible spoon* and *the bong-tree*. A runcible spoon is a kind of fork with two broad prongs and one sharp-edged, curved prong. She thinks they look like pudgy forks. Runcible spoons are perfect for eating pie a la mode. Runcible spoons can be purchased from antique dealers.

Brett has tried to imagine what a bong-tree looked like since she was a little girl and first heard the poem. When she was on Martinique, she found an interesting tree. Instead of leaves, the tree had long drooping fronds with little green balls hanging from them. She did not discover the tree's name, but she says it looks like the bong-tree she imagined as a child.

The pea-green boat in *The Owl and the Pussycat* is a gommier, and it is indigenous to the island of Martinique. The hull is made from a hollowed-out tree. A board is then attached to each side and reinforced with a strip of wood. Brett named the boat Promise because the Owl proposes (or promises his love) to the Pussycat. The model for the Pussycat was Priscilla, a pet cat belonging to Brett's mother.

The Pussycat wears the traditional dress of the island of Martinique—a white blouse with ruffles and lace, a plaid madras skirt with a starched petticoat, coral bead necklace, and a madras turban. According to custom, the turban was worn in a special way to tell admirers that the woman was single (one point up), had a beau (two points up), was married (three points up) or was married but loved attention (four points up). In Brett's book the Pussycat wears one point up until she marries the Owl. Then she wears three points up.

Flowers and straw patterns set against tropical skies above and fascinating underwater seascapes below adorn each two-page spread of *The Owl and the Pussycat*. As Owl and Pussycat sail off across the sea, another story unfolds in the clear water beneath the boat. One by one, exotic sea creatures swim into the picture, and a small yellow fish seems to be looking for someone special. *The Owl and the Pussycat* is an ALA Notable book.

Language Arts

1. Read *The Owl and the Pussycat.* Discuss words positioned above and below the pictures as you closely examine them. This book really contains two tales. The story of the Owl and Pussycat's courtship takes place upon the blue Caribbean Sea. But observant youngsters will spy a wordless tale developing beneath the waves as well. Have children describe events occuring below the surface of the water.

The Owl and the Pussycat (cont.)

Language Arts (cont.)

2. Fingerplay—**Five Little Seashells**

   Five little seashells lying on the shore,
   Swish went the waves and then there were four.
   Four little seashells pretty as could be,
   Swish went the waves and then there were three.
   Three little seashells all pearly new,
   Swish went the waves and then there were two.
   Two little seashells shining in the sun,
   Swish went the waves and then there was one.
   One little seashell left all alone,
   I picked it up and took it home.

3. Poem—**Wise Old Owl**

   A wise old owl sat in an oak.
   The more he heard, the less he spoke;
   The less he spoke, the more he heard.
   Why aren't we all like that wise old bird?

   Discuss the poem's meaning with the children. Ask them to explain why an owl is often described as wise.

4. Bloom's Taxonomy of Higher Order Questions:

   Knowledge—What color was the Owl's boat?
   Who married the Owl and the Pussycat?
   Comprehension—Why did the Owl want to buy the Pig's ring?
   Application—If you were going to be at sea for a year, what would you take to eat?
   Analysis—Tell all the reasons someone should go to sea for a year.
   Synthesis—How would the story have changed if the Pussycat refused to marry the Owl?
   Evaluation—Would you want to live at sea for a year? Why or why not?

Math/Science

1. Owl Facts—Show children pictures of real owls in the *Owl Zoobook*. Relate the following information to the children:
   - Owls have eyes on the fronts of their heads.
   - Owls see well in the dark.
   - Owls eat mice and harmful insects.
   - Owls are nocturnal—they sleep during the day and hunt at night.
   - Baby owls are called owlets.

2. Fish Facts—Show children pictures of fish or bring in a real fish. If possible, set up an aquarium. Share the following information with the children:
   - Fish have gills to breathe with.
   - Fish have two pairs of fins (like their arms and legs).
   - Fish have hard scales.
   - Fish use their tails to swim (like a boat's rudder and propeller combined).
   - Fish are cold-blooded animals with backbones.

The Owl and the Pussycat (cont.)

Math/Science (cont.)

4. Blue Wave—In a glass jar with a metal lid, combine turpentine and rubbing alcohol. Drop in blue food coloring. Roll jar back and forth to create ocean wave.

5. Sandy Beaches Workjobs—Glue sandpaper beaches onto blue poster board. Have children put seashells on sand or in water (counting/addition skills). This activity is an adaptation of workjobs from *Math Their Way.*

6. Tropical Flowers—Obtain a reference book on tropical flowers. Have students research the flowers appearing in the borders of Jan Brett's book.

7. Salt Water/Fresh Water Experiment—Have children taste fresh water. Explain that lakes contain this type of water. Allow children to taste salt water. Explain that oceans are made of this type of water. Ask children to describe the difference (i.e., one is salty). Do NOT describe the water as fresh or salty; just let them taste it.

8. Sand Castles—Place sand castle molds, buckets, and shovels in the texture table with wet sand. Allow children to build and construct with these materials.

9. Sorting Seashells—Purchase a variety of seashells from a craft store. Place a handful in the center of a sorting tray and encourage children to group similar shells together.

10. Seashell Patterns—Have children complete the seashell patterns begun on page 78 or create their own patterns using real shells.

Art

1. Lunch Sack Owls—Have children cut out construction paper eyes, triangle tufts, and ear tufts. Glue facial features and feathers onto lunch sack. Stuff with newspaper and tie shut.

2. Aquariums—Have children glue sand, aquarium stones, fish crackers, green tinted curly pasta (seaweed) and seashells onto a Styrofoam meat tray.

3. Fish—Allow children to fingerpaint or watercolor or create mosaics from pre-cut fish shapes. Encourage children to create two fish. Stuff fish and staple together. Hang fish from the ceiling with green crepe paper used as seaweed streamers.

4. Straw Mats—After listening to the story, have youngsters examine each of Jan Brett's borders. Ask them to describe what they see. For each student, fold a brown piece of construction paper in half. Have students cut on the lines drawn (use paper cutter or have them pre-cut for very young children). Unfold the paper and weave yellow strips in and out of the slits. Assist students, if necessary, in gluing the loose strip ends to the mat's margin. Glue colorful fish and seashells to the straw mat. Laminate and use as a placemat or give to parents as a special gift.

5. Underwater Worlds—Using fluorescent crayons, have each artist color underwater creatures and plants on white construction paper. Encourage thick applications of crayon. Blend a little yellow tempera paint into blue before thinning it to a watery consistency. Have students wash this over their pictures, using a wide brush.

 # 454 Favorite Authors: Jan Brett   74   *© 1995 Teacher Created Materials, Inc.*

The Owl and the Pussycat (cont.)

Art *(cont.)*

6. Bead Necklaces—Mix 2 cups (500 mL) flour, 1 cup (250 mL) salt, 1 cup (250 mL) water and 1 teaspoon (5 mL) cooking oil together. Tint play dough with food coloring (divide the dough before adding the color). Shape into small balls and push a toothpick through the center of each ball. Allow to dry, and then string onto yarn to make a necklace.

7. Tissue Paper Flower Necklace—Have children cut flower shapes from colored tissue paper (have shapes pre-cut for younger children). Thread onto a string, using a blunt needle. Alternate tissue paper flowers with straw sections or play-dough beads.

8. Sand Painting—Purchase colored sand from a craft store or tint sand with dry tempera. Have students draw a picture and outline it with a black marker. Apply glue to inside of the picture and sprinkle sand over it. Shake off excess and allow to dry.

9. Sand Sculpture—Let children place layers of colored sand in baby-food jars.

10. Sand Castles—Allow children to use small gelatin molds to create sand castles from the recipe below. Toothpicks and stir-sticks can be used for carving and shaping the sand castles. Attach small flags to toothpicks and insert into sand castles. Sprinkle with glitter or mix glitter into paste in the recipe.

    Sand Castle

    6 cups (1.5 L) sand

    1 cup (250 mL) dry wallpaper paste

    Mix dry sand and wallpaper paste. Add water until the sand has a clay-like consistency. It should be sticky and pack firmly. Wet sand will take longer to dry. Shape into a sand castle and allow to dry (three to five days). It will harden and become rock-like.

11. Seashell Border Frame—Cut a picture frame from heavy cardboard. Cut a square or rectangle shape out of the middle of the piece of cardboard. Have children glue on a variety of seashells around the cardboard border until it is completely covered. Tape a picture of the child in the space cut out. Attach a stand to support the picture when displayed. Picture and picture frame may be given as gifts to parents or grandparents.

Music

1. **"Wise Old Owl"**

   (tune: "Frere Jacques")

   Wise old owl, wise old owl,

   On the sea, on the sea,

   Who-oo are you winking at?

   Who-oo are you winking at?

   Is it she? Is it she?

2. "I'm a Little Fish" (song) in *Totline Theme-A-Saurus*, page 111.

© 1995 Teacher Created Materials, Inc.

The Owl and the Pussycat *(cont.)*

Movement

1. Ocean Waves

   A. Have children grasp the perimeter of a parachute and create gentle ocean waves with the fabric.

   B. Move to a cassette of ocean wave music, using streamers made from blue crepe paper, ribbon, or scarves.

Game

1. Whooo Is It? (listening skill)—One child is the mother owl. That child leaves the room while three owlets are selected. All of the children cover their mouths, but only the owlets say, "Whooo, whooo" while the mother owl searches for them.

Cooking

Gelatin Oceans

Sprinkle the bottom of a clear plastic cup with Cheerios. Top with green gelatin until the cup is half-full. Place gummy fish in the gelatin and add more green gelatin until the cup is full.

Sand Cups

2 cups (500 mL) cold milk

1 package (4-servings size) instant vanilla pudding

8 ounces (224 grams) thawed whipped topping

12 ounces (336 grams) crushed vanilla wafers

clear plastic cups

assorted decorations—e.g., miniature umbrellas, gummy fish, candy seashells, candy stars, chopped peanuts, candy rocks, etc.

Pour milk into a large bowl. Add pudding mix. Beat with whisk until well blended (one to two minutes). Let stand five minutes. Stir in whipped topping and half the crushed cookies. Place one tablespoon (15 mL) of crushed cookies into the bottom of the cups. Fill cups 3/4 full with pudding mixture. Top with remaining crushed cookies and/or peanuts. Refrigerate one hour and then decorate with candies.

Yield: 10 sand cups

 # 454 Favorite Authors: Jan Brett

The Owl and the Pussycat *(cont.)*

Cooking *(cont.)*

Owl Cookies

2 1/2 cups (625 mL) sifted flour

2 teaspoons (10 mL) baking powder

1/2 teaspoon (2 mL) salt

3/4 cup (187.5 mL) butter or margarine

1 cup (250 mL) firmly packed brown sugar

1 egg

1 teaspoon (5mL) vanillay extract

1 1/2 squares unsweetened chocolate, melted and cooled

1/2 teaspoon (2 mL) baking soda

semi-sweet chocolate chips

whole cashews

Sift flour with baking powder and salt. Cream butter in mixing bowl. Gradually add brown sugar; cream until light and fluffy. Add egg and vanilla extract and beat well. Blend in sifted dry ingredients gradually and mix thoroughly. Combine melted chocolate and soda. Remove two-thirds of dough to floured surface. Blend chocolate mixture into remaining dough and chill for easier handling. Roll out half of the plain dough to a 10" x 4 1/4" (25 cm x 11 cm) rectangle. Shape half the chocolate dough into a roll 10" (25 cm) long and place on rectangle of plain dough. Mold sides of plain dough around chocolate roll and wrap in waxed paper. Repeat with remaining dough. Chill at least two hours. Cut into slices 1/4" (.6 cm) thick. Place two slices side by side and touching on a greased cookie sheet to form an owl's face. Pinch a piece of dough on each slice to form ears. Place a chocolate piece in the center of each slice for eyes. Firmly press a whole cashew between slices for a beak. Bake at 350° F (180° C) for 8 – 12 minutes (until edges of cookie are a very light golden-brown). Remove from cookie sheets immediately and cool.

Yield: 4 dozen

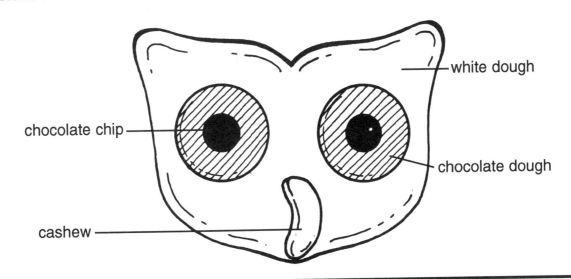

The Owl and the Pussycat

Seashell Patterns

Directions: Cut out the pictures at the bottom of the page. Glue a picture in the space provided to finish the pattern.

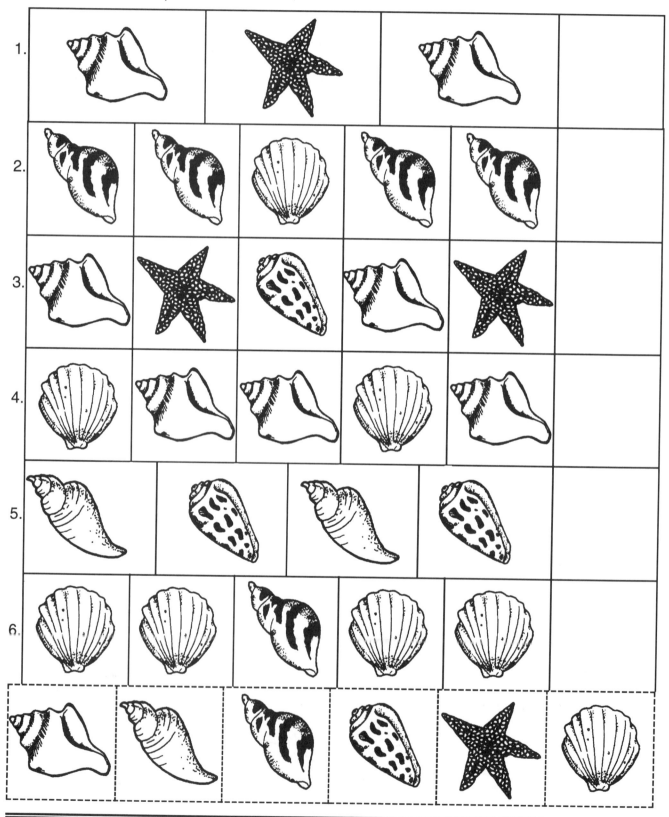

454 Favorite Authors: Jan Brett

Trouble with Trolls

Jan Brett's newest book is about a little girl named Treva who is confronted by trolls that want her dog for a pet. This feisty heroine is not only brave but quick-witted. Treva outsmarts one troll after another in this tale. From underground to mountain peak, Brett has filled this story with eye-catching detail. A new challenge awaits Treva as she gets closer and closer to the mountain top and nearer to losing Tuffi. The author's Siberian husky, Perky Pumpkin, served as the model for Tuffi. Keep your eyes on the little hedgehog working its way down to the trolls' underground home. (Maybe a dog is not the perfect pet after all!)

Language Arts

1. Read *Trouble With Trolls.* Discuss how Treva tricked the trolls. Allow children to talk about their own pets and special relationships with them. Ask children to think of an unusual animal they would like to have for a pet. Have them create a story about this unusual animal.

2. Bloom's Taxonomy of Higher Order Questions:

   Knowledge—What is the name of the dog in this story?

   Comprehension—Why did the trolls want Tuffi?

   Application—If it had been you, how would you have prevented the trolls from stealing Tuffi?

   Analysis—Compare Tuffi and the hedgehog. Which would make the best pet for a troll?

   Synthesis—How would the story have changed if Treva had been unable to outsmart the trolls?

   Evaluation—Which would you like to have as a pet—Tuffi, the hedgehog, or a troll? Why?

Math/Science

1. Winter Patterns—Children make patterns using pre-cut mitten, hat, sweater, boot and ski cutouts from page 83. Encourage them to create different patterns using these objects. Ask them to describe the pattern to you—for example, A, B, A, B . . . or hat, mitten, hat, mitten . . . .

2. Insulation Experiment—Discuss how clothes insulate us from the cold to keep us warmer. Test different materials to see which are the best insulators (those which keep either cold or heat out). Set out a bowl of ice cubes and a variety of insulation materials (e.g., tissue paper, aluminum foil, plastic wrap, fabric, newspaper, etc.) on the science table. Let the children tightly wrap each ice cube in a different material. Place each insulated ice cube and one uninsulated ice cube together in a bowl. (If you have five different insulators, you will need five bowls.) After an hour, have the children carefully unwrap the ice cubes and compare them to the uninsulated ice cube in each bowl. Which ice cube melted the most/least? Which insulation material worked the best? Discuss the reasons that Treva wanted her coat, sweater, mittens, hat, and boots returned.

© 1995 Teacher Created Materials, Inc.   79   # 454 Favorite Authors: Jan Brett

Trouble with Trolls *(cont.)*

Math/Science *(cont.)*

3. Hedgehog Information—Share the following facts with the children:
   - Hedgehogs are 9" (22.5 cm) long.
   - Hedgehogs have stiff hair that hardens into spines.
   - Hedgehogs roll into balls when they are in danger.
   - Hedgehogs are nocturnal.
   - Hedgehogs hibernate during the winter.
   - Hedgehogs eat insects, snakes, small animals, birds, and bird eggs.

Art

1. Trolls—Provide fake fur scraps and a variety of art materials for children to create their own trolls. Encourage them to make pets for their trolls also.
2. Crystallized Frost Pictures—Have students draw a winter scene on blue construction paper using white crayons. Put the picture through an epsom salt wash. When it dries, it will look like crystallized snow or frost.
3. Tuffi Tags—Children can create a dog tag for Tuffi using the salt dough recipe on page 62. Punch a hole in the dog tag and create a design on it prior to baking. If desired, food coloring can be used to tint the dog tag before baking it. After the dough is baked and cool, attach a leather shoestring to the hole. Children can use them for their pets or wear them as necklaces.
4. Trembling Trolls—Create an old-fashioned paperweight that is really a snowstorm in a jar. Use any small jar with a good lid, like those containing baby food. Carve a small troll from Styrofoam (or mold it from clay) or substitute a small toy—pine tree, snowman, tiny house, etc. Place the troll or toy inside the jar and glue it to the bottom. When it is dry, fill the jar with water to within 1/4 inch (.6 cm) of the top. Pour in some moth flakes for the "snow." Use a good waterproof glue or cement around the jar rim and lid, screw the lid on tightly, and let it dry completely. When all is dry, turn the jar upside down and watch the snowstorm!

Music

"Mitten Song"

(tune: "Skip to My Lou")

Thumbs in the thumb place, fingers all together,

This is the song we sing in mitten weather,

Doesn't matter whether, they're made of wool or leather,

Thumbs in the thumb place, fingers all together.

Game

Tuffi, Tuffi, Troll (like Duck, Duck, Goose)—"Tuffi" taps children on the head until she/he chooses another child to be the "Troll." "Troll" chases "Tuffi" who tries to get to the "Troll's" place on the circle before being caught by the "Troll." Any "Tuffi's" who are caught are taken to the "Troll's" underground home.

Trouble with Trolls (cont.)

Cooking

Troll Treats

1 cup (250 mL) chocolate chips

1 1/2 cups (375 mL) peanut butter

1/4 cup (62.5 mL) margarine

8-9 cups (1 L) mixed Chex cereal

1 box powdered sugar

Melt chocolate chips and peanut butter with margarine. Pour over mixed Chex in a large bowl. Put powdered sugar in large resealable bag and pour coated mixture into the bag. Shake until well coated with powdered sugar. Store in airtight container.

Gingerbread Trolls

1 package gingerbread mix

1/4 cup (62.5 mL) salad oil

1/4 cup (62.5 mL) milk

Pour the gingerbread mix into a large bowl. Add the milk and oil and mix with a spoon. Remove the dough from the bowl and shape it into a ball. Wrap the ball in plastic and refrigerate for one hour. After the dough has chilled, roll it out into a sheet 1/4" (.6 cm) thick. Cut out free-form shapes for trolls with pointed heads or other shapes if you prefer. (Patterns can be made for this or the children can design their own.) Place on greased cookie sheets and bake at 350° F (180° C) for 12 minutes. Allow to cool and decorate with icing for hair, raisins for eyes, etc.

Troll Soup

Make vegetable soup in a big black pot like the trolls.' Write recipe on chart paper as the children dictate it to you. Visit a grocery store and shop for the items needed to make the soup. Hang recipe near the writing table for children to copy (be sure to use rebus symbols or wrappers from items used on the chart for young children to read).

© 1995 Teacher Created Materials, Inc.   # 454 Favorite Authors: Jan Brett

Trouble with Trolls (cont.)

Cooking (cont.)

Treva's Tasty Graham Cracker House

This will look much like a gingerbread house covered with snow but will be much easier to make.

Materials

- graham crackers, eight squares for each student
- 1/2 pint-size (250 mL) milk cartons, clean and dry
- canned frosting
- small candies for decoration on the house
- miniature marshmallows
- dry cereal, various shapes
- craft sticks
- plastic knives
- ice cream cones
- stiff paper plates

Directions

Give each child eight squares of graham crackers, one clean milk carton, and a plastic knife. Place the milk carton on a sturdy paper plate. Using the frosting as mortar, students cover the sides and top of the carton with graham crackers, spreading the "mortar" with the plastic knives. Fill any empty spaces with mortar. The roof is a tricky part. You may have to help them hold the crackers in place a while until the frosting dries a bit.

Spread the roof with frosting and place marshmallows or cereal pieces onto it. Let some of the frosting drape from the roof eaves like icicles.

Near the house, stand an ice-cream cone upside down and cover with frosting to represent snow in tiered layers. (If you wish, green food coloring in the frosting may be used for the tree's first coat, followed by a covering of the white "snow" frosting. For the last touch, a pair of craft sticks with an outline of frosting may be leaned up against the house to represent Treva's skis.

#454 Favorite Authors: Jan Brett © 1995 Teacher Created Materials, Inc.

Trouble with Trolls

Winter Patterns

Directions: Cut apart cards and create patterns with winter items shown.

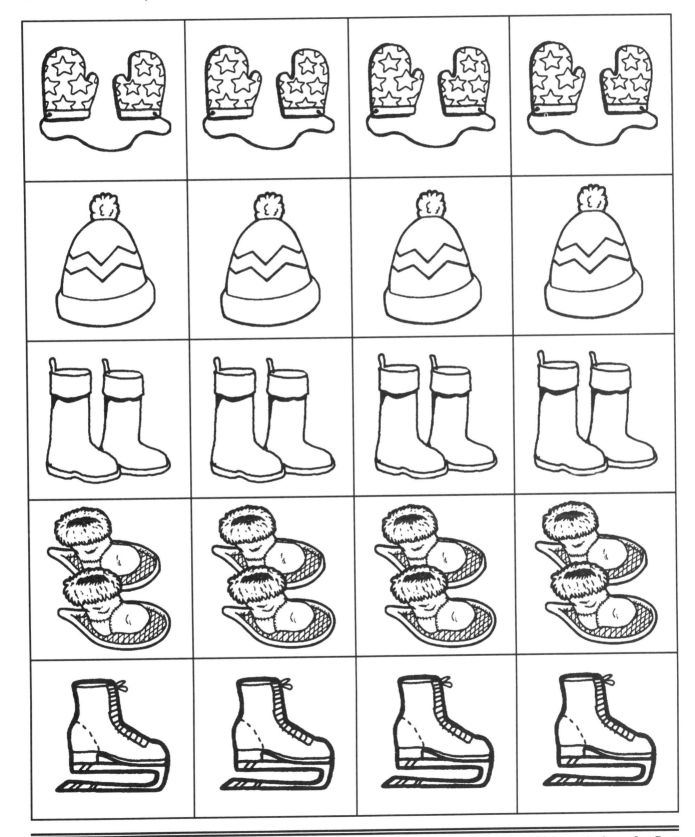

Fritz and the Beautiful Horses

Fritz and the Beautiful Horses marked Jan Brett's debut as an author. She first became interested in drawing horses after seeing the famous Lippizan stallions of Vienna on their first tour of the United States. Brett's full-color illustrations sparkle in intricate detail across every page of this exceptional picture book about Fritz, a sure-footed pony who finally gets the chance to shine in his own best way.

Language Arts

1. Prior to reading *Fritz and the Beautiful Horses*, ask children to define the word *beautiful* and have them identify the beautiful horses. Which one do they think is Fritz? Why? Is he beautiful? Why or why not?

2. Read *Fritz and the Beautiful Horses*. Ask children to define the word *beautiful* now. Is Fritz a beautiful horse? Why or why not? (Note: Some young children may not yet understand that beauty is not always judged by outward appearance; this is an opportunity to introduce the concept.)

3. Read the book *All the Pretty Horses,* written and illustrated by Susan Jeffers.

4. Border Artwork—No borders appear in the illustrations of *Fritz and the Beautiful Horses*. The author probably had not begun to use the story-within-the-story device yet. Jan Brett says she uses the borders when she has too many ideas for one story. Observant children will notice that the borders are missing in this story. Ask them to explain why Fritz's story is center stage in this book.

5. Bloom's Taxonomy of Higher Order Questions:

   Knowledge—What was the hero's name in the story?

   Comprehension—Why wasn't Fritz allowed into the walled city?

   Application—If you had been a citizen of the walled city, would you have allowed Fritz inside?

   Analysis—Compare and contrast Fritz with the beautiful horses.

   Synthesis—How would the story have changed if the bridge had not cracked when it did, thus stranding the children?

   Evaluation—Do you think Fritz or the beautiful horses were more suited for children to ride? Why?

Math/Science

1. Horse Information—Ask a veterinarian to visit and discuss how to care for a horse. If possible, visit a farm with horses. Display pictures, grooming tools, and models of horses on the science table.

2. Blacksmith Demonstration—Visit a blacksmith to see how horseshoes are fashioned.

3. Counting—Count the number of horses on any page within the text.

 # 454 Favorite Authors: Jan Brett   *© 1995 Teacher Created Materials, Inc.*

Fritz and the Beautiful Horses (cont.)

Art

1. Create-a-Horse, of Course!—Children bring recycled materials—e.g., boxes, toilet paper or paper towel tubes, egg cartons, berry baskets, milk jugs, etc. Put scissors, masking tape, fake fur, yarn, crayons, markers, paint, construction paper, glue, Styrofoam pieces, etc., on the art table. Children are to create horse sculptures. Section off part of the room as a corral. Place horse sculptures inside the corral.
2. Castles—Allow children to create castle structures out of toilet paper tubes, paper towel tubes, milk cartons, egg cartons, cardboard boxes, large and small paper cups, foam carry-out boxes, etc. Each child will need a piece of Styrofoam packing material for a base. Egg cartons can be placed around the base to form walls. Almost any recycled item can be used. Let your imagination run!

Music

"Hush Little Baby"
(traditional lullaby)
Hush little baby, don't say a word,
Momma's gonna buy you a mockingbird.
If that mockingbird don't sing,
Momma's gonna buy you a diamond ring.
If that diamond ring turns to brass,
Momma's gonna buy you a looking-glass.
If that looking-glass gets broke,
Momma's gonna buy you a billy goat.
If that billy goat gets bony,
Momma's gonna buy you a Shetland pony.
If that pony runs away,
Ta-ra-ra-ra-boom-de-ay.

"Clippity, Clippity, Clop"
(tune: "Hickory, Dickory, Dock")
Clippity, clippity, clop,
The horses go clippity, clop,
They gallop and gallop,
They start and they stop,
Clippity, clippity, clop.

Mairzey Doats
Mairzey doats and dozey doats
(Mares eat oats and does eat oats)
And little lambsey divey,
(And little lambs eat ivy)
A kidley divey too, wouldn't you?
(A kid will eat ivy too, wouldn't you?)

Fritz and the Beautiful Horses *(cont.)*

Music *(cont.)*

"All the Pretty Little Horses"
(See bibliography, page 112.)

Hushaby, don't you cry,

Go to sleep, little lady,

When you wake, you shall have,

All the pretty little horses.

Blacks and bays, dapples and grays,

All the pretty little horses,

Hushaby, don't you cry,

Go to sleep, little lady.

Movement

1. "Ride and Swing" from *Sally the Swinging Snake* by Hap Palmer (Booklet inside of album includes directions and words.)
2. Block Corner—Children build a walled city, using various sizes of hollow and solid wooden blocks and/or cardboard blocks.
3. Dramatic Play—Corral (borrow saddles or create them from folded blankets to set up on blocks for children to ride; children create a block fence for the corral).

Game

Horseshoes (good eye-hand coordination activity).

454 Favorite Authors: Jan Brett © 1995 Teacher Created Materials, Inc.

Fritz and the Beautiful Horses *(cont.)*

Cooking

Haystacks

6 ounces (180 g) butterscotch chips

1/2 cup (125 mL) peanut butter

6 ounces (180 g) chow mein noodles

Melt butterscotch chips and peanut butter. Mix in chow mein noodles. Drop by spoonfuls onto waxed-paper-lined cookie sheet. Refrigerate until mixture sets up (about 15 minutes).

Fritz's Favorite Cookies

2 1/4 cups (563 mL) butter or margarine

2 1/4 cups (563 mL) white sugar

2 1/2 cups (625 mL) brown sugar

5 eggs

2 1/2 teaspoons (12 mL) vanilla

4 1/2 cups (1.1 L) flour

2 1/4 teaspoons (11 mL) baking soda

1 1/8 teaspoons (5 mL) baking powder

1 1/8 teaspoons (5 mL) salt

4 1/2 cups (1.1 L) rolled oats

12 ounces (360 g) chocolate chips

1 cup (250 mL) chopped walnuts

Cream butter, sugars, eggs, and vanilla. Sift together flour, baking soda, baking powder and salt. Add to creamed mixture. Mix in rolled oats. When everything is well mixed, add chocolate chips and walnuts. Using an ice-cream scoop, drop batter onto a greased cookie sheet and bake at 350° F (180° C) until lightly brown on edges and chewy in the middle (about 15 minutes). Do not overbake or cookies will be tough.

Yield: 4 dozen

Life Skill—Discrimination

Discuss the fact that Fritz was discriminated against (he was not allowed into the walled city) because he was not considered beautiful. Everyone must be accepted for who they are and what they can contribute. We are all different in some way, and we all have been given different talents. Read *We Are All Alike . . . We Are All Different*. Discuss how we are alike and different. Write a class big book about how Fritz and the beautiful horses are alike and different. Have children illustrate the book, laminate it, and place the class creation in the book corner.

The Valentine Bears

Jan Brett has served as illustrator for quite a few books written by other authors. Her bear illustrations in this story are reminiscent of those in *Goldilocks and the Three Bears* and *Berlioz the Bear*. Mr. Bear is modeled after Brett's husband, Joseph Hearne. His better half, Mrs. Bear, is none other than Brett herself! And if the Ukrainian costumes look familiar, it is because they are similar to those in *The Mitten*. Young readers will be delighted with the surprise that is in store for both bears as they celebrate their first Valentine's Day. Jan Brett's finely textured illustrations convey the spirit of the holiday in a book that should be shared in every early childhood classroom.

Language Arts

1. Read *The Valentine Bears*. Discuss fully the poems written by Mrs. Bear. Read a variety of poems to the children. Introduce or review rhyming words with the class. Say a word and have children supply all the words that rhyme with the original one.

2. Poetry Writing—Write a class poem with the children. Encourage older students to write their own poems following this group activity.

3. Sign Language—Teach the children to sign the following phrases:

   A. **I love you**.

   I—point index finger at yourself.

   love—Cross fists over heart area of chest.

   you—Point to person the message is directed towards with your index finger.

   Variation: Extend the thumb, index, and pinkie fingers while other fingers remain in fist position. The letters "I", "L" and "Y" from the message "I love you" are displayed.

   B. **Be my Valentine.**

   Be—Place "B" handshape (four fingers together with thumb bent on palm) at mouth. Move your hand straight out.

   my—Place your hand flat against your chest, indicating possession.

   Valentine—Using the third finger of each hand, draw an outline of a heart over the heart area of the chest.

   C. **Hugs and kisses**

   Hugs—Both hands form fists and move towards the chest in a hugging motion.

   and—Open right hand grabs air toward left side of the body. As you pull the hand across your chest, the handshape closes until all fingers are touching (do not form a fist).

   kisses—Fingertips of the right hand touch your lips and then your right cheek.

 # 454 Favorite Authors: Jan Brett   *© 1995 Teacher Created Materials, Inc.*

The Valentine Bears *(cont.)*

Language Arts *(cont.)*

4. Bloom's Taxonomy of Higher Order Questions:

    Knowledge—What gift did Mr. Bear give to Mrs. Bear?

    Comprehension—Why did Mrs. Bear want to celebrate Valentine's Day with Mr. Bear?

    Application—If you had to wake a sound sleeper like Mr. Bear, how would you go about it?

    Analysis—Compare the two poems written by Mrs. Bear. How are they alike/different?

    Synthesis—How would the story have changed if Mrs. Bear's alarm clock had not gone off?

    Evaluation—Which poem did you like best? Why?

Math/Science

1. Bear Facts—Show children real pictures of bears from the *Zoobook*. Share the following information with them:
    - Bears eat insects and honey.
    - Some bears do not truly hibernate—they sleep on cold winter days and forage for food on warm winter days.
    - Bears are warm-blooded.
    - Bears are mammals.
    - Bear babies are born live.

2. Hibernation—Discuss which animals sleep all winter long. Teach children the new vocabulary word *hibernate*. Do all bears truly hibernate?

3. Bees and Honey—Discuss the bee community (queen, drone, worker, guard) and each one's job in the hive. Show the children a beehive. Invite a beekeeper to explain how bees make honey. Use a faceted magnifying viewer to simulate a bee's eye. Allow children to look through the viewer and describe what they see. An excellent source for factual information on bees and the honey-making process is *Honeybees* by Barrie Watts. As a concluding activity, taste different varieties of honey and graph the children's favorite type.

4. Calendar—Count the months from October 14 to February 14. Count the number of days from February 14 until spring (March 21).

5. Clocks—Begin learning how to tell time. The bears' clock had months and days on it. Discuss the characteristics of real clocks. Let the student gathering-circle represent a gigantic clock for young children and discuss what happens each hour at school. Refer to the activity sheets on pages 93 - 94 for skill practice.

6. Seasons—Compare and contrast the seasons of winter and spring on the activity sheet provided (page 95). Young children may depict the seasons visually, while older children may choose to describe the seasons.

© 1995 Teacher Created Materials, Inc.

The Valentine Bears (cont.)

Art

1. Illustrators—Give each child a copy of the poem written by the class. Older children can copy it from a chart. Ask children to illustrate or draw the pictures for this poem.

2. Create a valentine for Mom and/or Dad—Place a variety of objects on the art table—e.g., doilies, stickers, glue, glitter, yarn, foam shapes, markers, stamps, stamp pads, etc. Encourage the children to make a valentine from the materials available.

3. Texture Rubbings—Discuss the texture of Jan Brett's illustrations and how it makes them look real. Encourage children to take rubbings from a variety of objects (carpet, brick wall, wood, tree trunk, headstone, asphalt, etc.) to see whether they look real.

4. "Heart Prints"—Children use a variety of objects to make prints on red construction paper hearts. Prints can be made from sponges, empty thread spools, fingers, kitchen utensils, fruits and vegetables, etc. Dip objects in either white or pink paint for prints.

5. Hibernating Bears—Tear a half-circle from the rim of a Styrofoam cup. Turn the cup over and glue to a paper plate. Glue brown pompons to the plate inside the cup (cave). Don't wake these bears until spring!

6. Winter Scenes—Children draw winter scenes on blue construction paper. Dip pictures in epsom salt wash. When dry, frost will appear.

7. Springtime Flowers—Have the students make daffodils, pussy willows, forsythia, and cherry blossoms.

   (For daffodils and pussy willows, see directions on page 53.)

   Forsythia—Students draw brown branches on white construction paper. Bunch yellow tissue paper squares into blossom shapes and glue onto the branches.

   Cherry Blossoms—Tint popcorn red (shake it in a bag with dry red tempera paint). The students draw trees and glue on the "cherry blossoms."

8. Heart-Shaped Tissue Paper Collage Pin—Purchase small wooden hearts. Sand the edges. Cut various shapes of pink tissue paper into squares. Thin glue with water. Have the students brush on glue and place a layer of tissue paper over the glue. Continue until about six layers are on the wood shape. Dry completely and spray with lacquer. Use hot glue to attach a safety catch pin. Pins and wooden shapes can be purchased at most craft stores.

9. Bear's Cave—Children can decorate a large cardboard box with brown, green, and black paint, real leaves and twigs. Cut an opening for children to crawl through and place in a dramatic play corner.

Music

1. "Skinnamarink" on *One Elephant, Deux Elephants* by Sharon, Lois and Bram
2. "Big Red Hearts" (song) in Jan/Feb 1989, *Totline* (Vol. 11, Issue 1) page 19.

The Valentine Bears (cont.)

Dramatic Play—Bear's Cave

Place bear caves created by the children in the center of the room. Encourage children to pretend they are bears. Face painting materials should be available for their use.

Game

    A Valentine, a Valentine

    (similar to A Tisket, a Tasket)

    A valentine, a valentine,

    A red and white valentine,

    I sent a valentine to my friend,

    And on the way I lost it, I lost it.

Children say the verse with teacher. One child skips around the circle and drops the valentine behind another child who then runs to catch the giver. The original child tries to get back to his/her place in the circle.

Cooking

Heart-Shaped Sugar Cookies

2 1/4 cups (563 mL) sifted flour

1/4 teaspoon (1 mL) salt

2 teaspoons (10 mL) baking powder

1/2 cup (125 mL) butter or margarine

1 cup (250 mL) sugar

2 eggs, beaten

1/2 teaspoon (2 mL) vanilla

1 tablespoon (15 mL) milk

Sift dry ingredients together. Cream butter and sugar. Add eggs and vanilla to creamed mixture and then stir in dry ingredients. Add milk. Roll out dough to 1/4" (.6 cm) thick and cut with heart-shaped cookie cutters. Sprinkle with red and pink sugar crystals. Bake at 350° F (180° C) for 12 minutes.

Yield: 2 1/2 dozen

The Valentine Bears (cont.)

Cooking (cont.)

Honey Butter

Mix one part honey to two parts butter. Spread on bread or biscuits for a sweet-tasting snack.

Honey Cookies

- 2 1/4 cups (563 mL) sifted flour
- 1 teaspoon (5 mL) baking soda
- 1/4 teaspoon (1 mL) salt
- 1/2 teaspoon (2 mL) cinnamon
- 1/2 cup (125 mL) softened butter or margarine
- 1 cup (250 mL) honey
- 1/2 cup (125 mL) brown sugar
- 2 eggs, well beaten
- 1 1/2 cups (375 mL) raisins
- 1/2 cup (125 mL) chopped walnuts

Sift flour, soda, salt and spice together. Cream butter and brown sugar. Stir honey into creamed mixture. Add eggs, then dry ingredients. Stir in raisins and walnuts. Mix thoroughly. Drop from teaspoon onto greased baking sheet. Bake at 350° F (180° C) for 12–15 minutes.

Yield: 4 dozen

Chocolate Covered Critters

- 6 ounces (180 g) chocolate chips
- 6 ounces (180 g) butterscotch chips
- 3 ounce (90 g) can chow mein noodles
- 8 ounces (240 g) peanuts

Melt chips. Add noodles and peanuts. Mix well. Drop onto waxed-paper cookie sheet and cool in refrigerator until mixture sets up.

---

454 Favorite Authors: Jan Brett   92   © 1995 Teacher Created Materials, Inc.

The Valentine Bears

Large Clock

Directions: Duplicate as many as needed. Cut out clock hands and attach to clock, using a paper fastener.

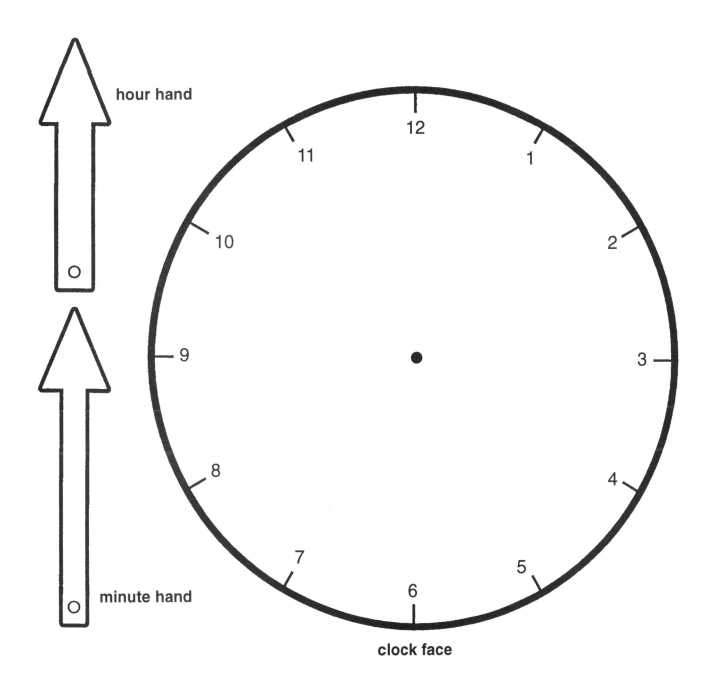

© 1995 Teacher Created Materials, Inc. — # 454 Favorite Authors: Jan Brett

The Valentine Bears

Telling Time

Directions: Cut out the times at the bottom of the page. To show what time it is, glue each time in the box under the correct clocks.

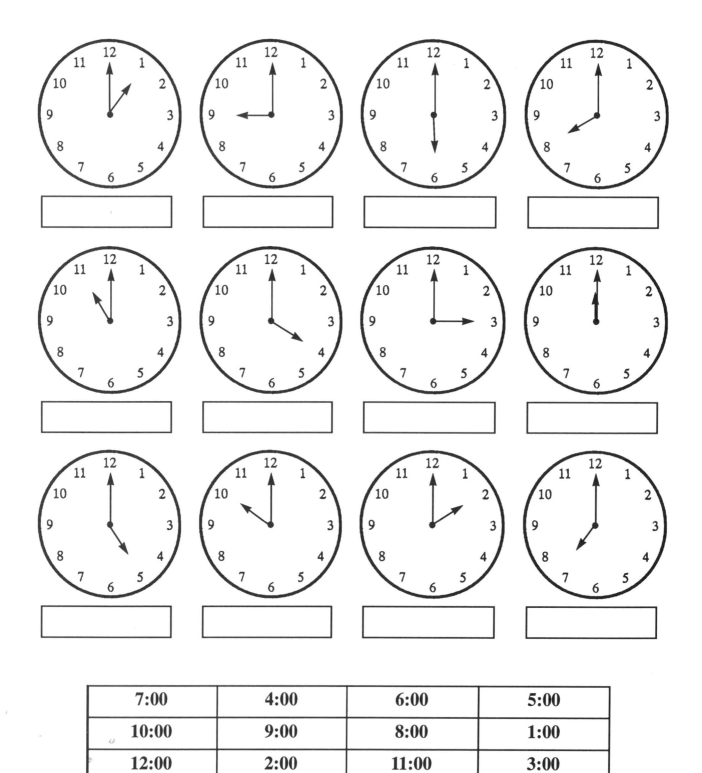

454 Favorite Authors: Jan Brett © 1995 Teacher Created Materials, Inc.

The Valentine Bears

Seasons

Winter is…

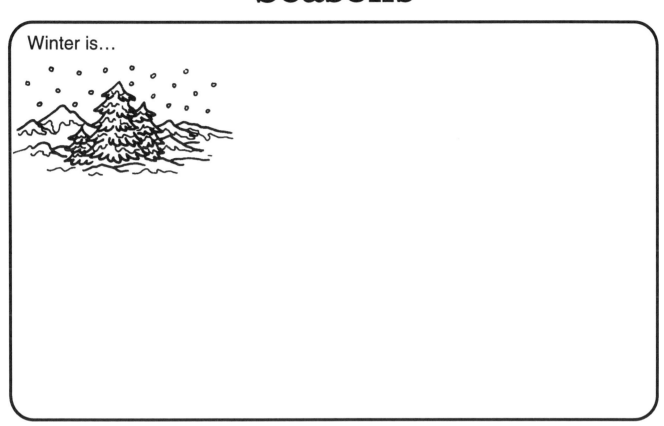

Spring is…

The Mother's Day Mice

The adorable mice in this tale are remarkably reminiscent of those in *Goldilocks and the Three Bears* and *The Mitten*. And there is a very good reason for the similarity. Once again, Jan Brett's pet, Little Pearl, was the model for the three mouse brothers.

The three mice in this story search the meadow near their home for the perfect Mother's Day gifts. The big brother picks a fluffy, white "wish flower" (dandelion), and the middle brother finds a ripe, juicy strawberry. The little brother has his heart set on picking honeysuckle (my own mother's favorite!), but a large, black cat standing guard prevents his access to the flowering bush.

In this delightfully illustrated tale, the three brothers discover the magic of love and sharing within a warm family atmosphere. The animals are so real you can practically see their whiskers twitch. Jan Brett has even managed to make acorns come alive by giving them facial features. Although the book has no borders, if you look closely you will discover a menagerie of animals and insects hidden among the meadow grasses.

Jan Brett's beautifully wrought illustrations convey the spirit of love in a book that should be shared with young children close to the date of this all-important holiday.

Language Arts

1. Prediction—Display the cover of *The Mother's Day Mice*. Ask children to predict what the story is going to be about.

2. Read *The Mother's Day Mice*. Ask the students which gift they think is most important and why.

3. Discussion—Reread *The Mother's Day Mice*. Point out each time the little mouse is afraid. Ask children if they are ever afraid of anything and, if so, of what. Relate a childhood fear to the children. Ask them if they were ever frightened of something but are not anymore. How did they learn not to be afraid of it?

4. Sharing—Right before Mother Mouse blows the fluffy dandelion seeds, she makes a wish. Ask students to share times when they made wishes (birthday party, first star of the night, falling star, prayer, etc.). Have each child write or dictate two to three wishes.

5. Bloom's Taxonomy of Higher Order Questions:

   Knowledge—List the gift each mouse wanted to bring home for Mother.

   Comprehension—Why couldn't Little Mouse pick some honeysuckle?

   Application—If it were you, what would you bring home as a gift for your mother?

   Analysis—What parts of the story could not have happened in the real world?

   Synthesis—How would the story have changed if the cat had not been at Honeysuckle Cottage?

   Evaluation—Which gift do you think Mother Mouse liked best? Why?

The Mother's Day Mice (cont.)

Math/Science

1. Mouse Facts—Share the following facts about mice with the class:
   - Mice are the smallest rodents.
   - Mice are mammals (their babies are born live, they have fur, they drink their mother's milk).
   - Mice use their front teeth for gnawing.
   - Mice are plant-eaters, but house mice will eat just about anything.
   - A mouse's enemy is any animal that eats meat.
   - An excellent source of information on these cute little rodents is *Discovering Rats and Mice* by Jill Bailey.

2. Size Seriation—Children sort a variety of real objects into small, medium, and large groups (e.g., pizza boxes, chairs, balls, gift boxes, books, etc.). Complete page 100 as a review of this skill.

3. Graphing—After sampling various types of cheese, have students graph their favorite.

Art

1. Fluff Balls—Children re-create the Biggest Mouse's gift by tracing (use a plastic lid) and cutting a construction paper circle. To decorate, glue on cotton or dot on white paint, using a Q-tip. If the circle is dark blue or black, a Q-tip dipped in bleach and dotted on the paper will create an interesting effect. Attach a green stem to the fluff ball. Display on a bulletin board with the children's wishes (see Language Arts activity #4).

2. Mother Portraits—Childen draw pictures of their mothers on white construction paper. Ask them to write or dictate a few sentences about their mothers and why they love them. Mount pictures on colored construction paper, being sure to leave 2" (5 cm) borders. Encourage the children to decorate the borders with glitter, designs, embossing, rubber stamps, etc. Create a bulletin board display of these "masterpieces."

3. Heart Mouse—Each child folds paper in half and cuts a half-heart design on the fold:

   Draw an eye and whiskers on each side of the mouse and glue a yarn tail to the other end.

4. Mother's Day Gift—Select one of the following ideas to make as a gift for this special holiday:

   A. Handprint Heart Wallhanging—Fold over 1" (2.5 cm) on one side of a 16" x 16" (40 cm x 40 cm) sheet of white muslin and stitch a hem in the bottom of the fold. A dowel rod will slide through this when the hanging is completed. Lightly draw a heart shape in the middle of the fabric with a pencil. Using fabric paint, students place handprints around the heart shape, covering the pencil outline. When the paint is dry, slide a dowel through the hem and attach ribbon to dowel ends for hanging.

The Mother's Day Mice *(cont.)*

Art *(cont.)*

B. Placemat—Each child sponge-paints, rubber-stamps, or texture-rubs a design on a piece of light, construction paper. When the design is dry, laminate.

C. Tissue Paper Collage Pin—Sand pre-cut wood shapes. Cut squares of tissue paper. Thin glue with water. Child brushes on a layer of glue and covers it with tissue paper. Continue until about six layers have been put on the wooden shape. When dry, spray with lacquer. Use hot glue to attach a safety-catch pin on the back. Pins and wooden shapes can be purchased at most craft stores.

5. Mother's Day Card—Fold a piece of construction paper in half. Fold it again and once again. Eight boxes will now be visible when the paper is opened. Cut rectangle shapes from old wallpaper books to fit inside the boxes. Have children glue on the wallpaper shapes so the front of each card resembles a patchwork quilt. Inside the cards have students write a Mother's Day message (for young children, you may wish to have something like "Happy Mother's Day!" pre-written on the inside of the card). Children may attach a school picture to the card (many photo companies supply free service strips of each child). Glue the following poem on the inside of the card:

> *Our family's like a patchwork quilt,*
>
> *With kindness gently sewn;*
>
> *Each piece is an original,*
>
> *With beauty of its own.*
>
> *With threads of warmth and happiness,*
>
> *It's tightly stitched together,*
>
> *To last in love throughout the years;*
>
> *Our family is forever.*

6. Over in the Meadow—Place over-in-the-meadow background patterns on a large bulletin board to create a setting for student-created stories. Let individual students place pattern creatures in appropriate places on the bulletin board (fish in pond or stream, bird in tree or nest, etc.) Then encourage the students to use their heart-mice to "travel" from place to place around the meadow as they tell stories based on *The Mother's Day Mice* but with any variations they may wish to add.

Music

1. "Skinnamarink" on *One Elephant, Deux Elephants* by Sharon, Lois and Bram.
2. "Over in the Meadow" on *The Musical Munkins Are . . . Makin' Music.*

The Mother's Day Mice (cont.)

Cooking

1. Cheese Tasting Party—Sample a variety of cheeses and have each child vote for his/her favorite kind.
2. Strawberry Pie—Have students wash, hull, and slice strawberries (with adult supervision). Mix with strawberry glaze and fill pre-made tart or pie shells.
3. Strawberry Shortcake—Have students wash, hull, and slice strawberries (with adult supervision). Spoon strawberries over biscuits baked by the students.
4. Mouse Cupcakes—Bake cupcakes according to package directions. Frost with white icing. Stand up two Oreo cookies for ears. Place two chocolate chips (eyes), a gumdrop (nose) and black licorice (whisker) in appropriate places.
5. Sugar Cookies—Bake sugar cookies for the Mother's Day Open House.

Sugar Cookies

2 1/4 cups (563 mL) sifted flour

1/4 (1 mL) teaspoon salt

2 teaspoons (10 mL) baking powder

1/2 cup (125 mL) butter or margarine

1 cup (250 mL) sugar

2 eggs, beaten

1/2 teaspoon (2 mL) vanilla

1 tablespoon (15 mL) milk

Sift dry ingredients together. Cream butter and sugar. Add eggs and vanilla to creamed mixture and then stir in dry ingredients. Add milk. Roll out dough to 1/4" (.6 cm) thick and cut with desired cookie cutters. Sprinkle with sugar crystals. Bake at 350° F (180° C) for 12 minutes.

Yield: 2 1/2 dozen

Special Event—Mother's Day Open House

Invite mothers to a one-hour Open House the Friday before Mother's Day. Read *The Mother's Day Mice* or *Is Your Mama a Llama?* by Deborah Guarino. Have children assist in telling "Over in the Meadow." Color, cut, and laminate animals and numbered backgrounds (see pages 102–105). Pass out two to three characters to each child. While everyone sings the verses (see page 101 for one version), children place animals on the appropriately numbered background.

Serve punch and the sugar cookies made by the children. Children can present their mothers with the cards, portraits, and gifts they made for them.

The Mother's Day Mice

Size Seriation

Directions: Arrange each group of objects by size. Sort objects into small, medium, and large groups.

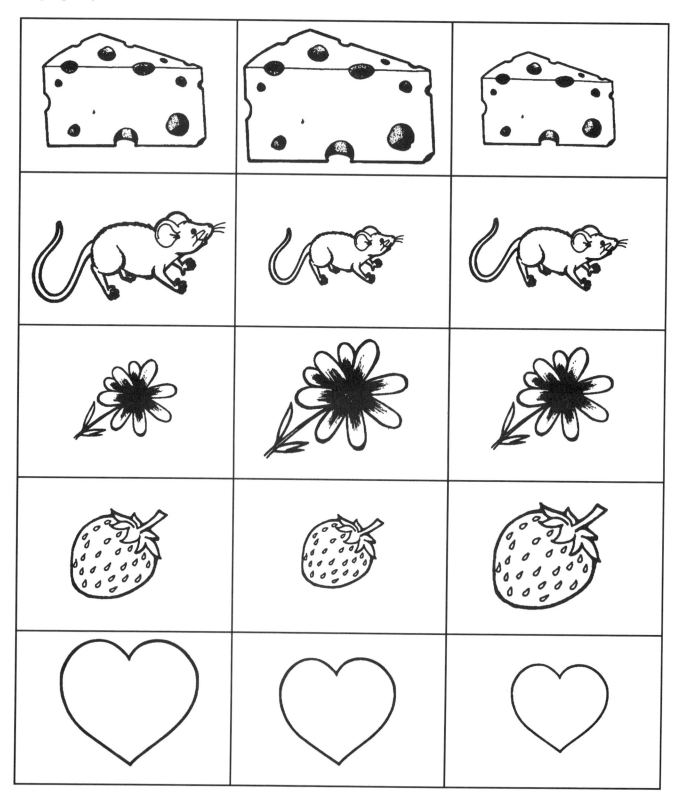

454 Favorite Authors: Jan Brett   100   © 1995 Teacher Created Materials, Inc.

The Mother's Day Mice

"Over in the Meadow"

These verses represent one version of a traditional Southern Appalachian counting rhyme, dating back to the 1800s. It has been attributed to Oliver A. Wadsworth.

Over in the meadow, in the sand, in the sun
Lived an old mother turtle and her little turtle one.
"Dig!" said the mother.
"I dig!" said the one.
So he dug all day,
In the sand, in the sun.

Over in the meadow, where the stream runs blue,
Lived an old mother fish and her little fishes two.
"Swim!" said the mother.
"We swim!" said the two.
So they swam and they swam,
Where the stream runs blue.

Over in the meadow, in a hole in a tree,
Lived a mother bluebird and her little birdies three.
"Sing!" said the mother.
"We sing!" said the three.
So they sang and they sang,
In the hole in the tree.

Over in the meadow, in the reeds on the shore,
Lived a mother muskrat and her litle ratties four.
"Dive!" said the mother.
"We dive!" said the four.
So they dived and they burrowed in the reeds on the shore.

Over in the meadow, in a snug beehive,
Lived a mother honeybee and her little honeys five.
"Buzz!" said the mother.
"We buzz!" said the five.
So they buzzed and they buzzed,
Near the snug beehive.

"Over in the Meadow" *(cont.)*

Over in the meadow, in a nest of sticks,
Lived a gray mother owl and her little owls six.
"Hoot!" said the mother.
"We hoot!" said the six.
So they hooted and they hooted
In their nest of sticks.

Over in the meadow, where the grass is like heaven,
Lived a white mother duck and her little duckies seven.
"Quack!" said the mother.
"We quack!" said the seven.
So they quacked and they quacked,
In the grass soft as heaven.

Over in the meadow, by the old mossy gate,
Lived a brown mother lizard and her little lizards eight.
"Bask!" said the mother.
"We bask!" said the eight.
So they basked in the sun,
By the old mossy gate.

Over in the meadow, where the clear pond shines,
Lived a green mother frog and her littles froggies nine.
"Croak!" said the mother.
"We croak!" said the nine.
So they croaked and they jumped,
Where the clear pond shines.

Over in the meadow, in a cool shady den,
Lived a red mother fox and her little foxes ten.
"Bark!" said the mother.
"We bark!" said the ten.
So they barked and they barked,
By the cool, shady den.

The Mother's Day Mice

Over-in-the-Meadow Background Patterns

Note: Enlarge pattern onto 14" x 17" (32 cm x 42.5 cm) pieces of colored construction paper. Glue or write numbers on each background before laminating them.

The Mother's Day Mice

Over-in-the-Meadow Patterns

The Mother's Day Mice

Over-in-the-Meadow Patterns *(cont.)*

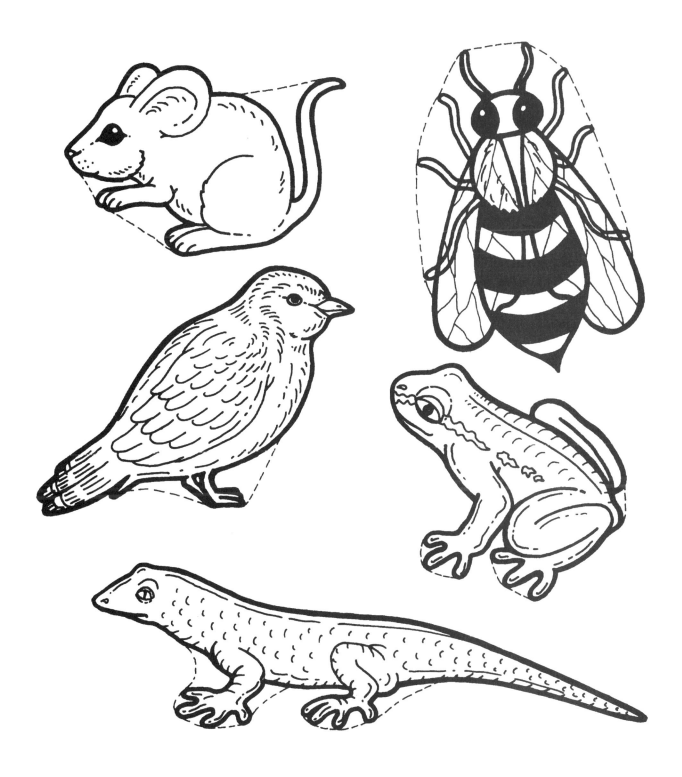

Beauty and the Beast

Folklore and fairy tales have captured the imagination of Jan Brett since she was a little girl. In her interpretation of *Beauty and the Beast*, she wanted a fairy to actually appear since it was her spell which set in motion the story events. Her beast, a wild boar, is modeled on the work of the nineteenth-century illustrator Walter Crane. The tapestries were inspired by designs from the William Morris Company. Brett's interpretation, which is based on Sir Author Quiller-Couch's version of the tale, includes mottos on the tapestries; Quiller-Couch displayed his messages over doorways and in dreams.

Language Arts

1. Read *Beauty and the Beast*. Read other versions of this tale. Compare and contrast them with Jan Brett's interpretation.

2. Reread *Beauty and the Beast*. Read each tapestry message and discuss its meaning.

3. Adjective Word Bank—Have students create a word bank of adjectives from *Beauty and the Beast*.

4. Bloom's Taxonomy of Higher Order Questions:

   Knowledge—What did Beauty ask her father to bring her?

   Comprehension—Why did Beauty have to go to the Beast's castle to live?

   Application—If you had been Beauty, what gift would you have asked your father for?

   Analysis—Compare and contrast Jan Brett's version of *Beauty and the Beast* with the classic Disney video version of the tale.

   Synthesis—How would the story have changed if Beauty had not returned to the Beast's castle?

   Evaluation—Which version of *Beauty and the Beast* do you like better—Jan Brett's or Disney's? Why?

Math/Science

1. Globe—Discuss the globe and how to use it. Map-reading skills may also be taught in conjunction with this.

2. Animal Study—Study any of the animals pictured within the story (boar, peacock, monkey, dog, deer, wolf, etc.). Students can research and write reports on these animals, either in small groups or independently.

3. Gardening—Plant flower seeds and predict the number of days until a sprout appears. Create miniature flower gardens from the plants. Study the importance of sunlight, water, and soil to plant growth. Demonstrate the effects when one of these factors is omitted. Have four test plants available. One receives sunlight and water. The second plant receives only sunlight, while the third is placed in a dark location but is regularly watered. The fourth one is completely neglected. Observe the plants over a two to four-week period and document the children's observations.

 # 454 Favorite Authors: Jan Brett 106 *© 1995 Teacher Created Materials, Inc.*

Beauty and the Beast *(cont.)*

Math/Science *(cont.)*

4. Favorite Fruit Graph—Ask each child to bring a favorite fruit to class. Prepare labels with the fruit name listed and a picture of the fruit on it (you can create stand-up labels simply by folding a piece of paper in half). Each child places his/her fruit in front of the appropriate label. Discuss the graph with the children, asking open-ended questions like "What can you tell me about the graph?"

Art

1. Peacock Painting—Children paint with "peacock" green and "peacock" blue paints. This can be done with watercolors, fingerpaint, dry tempera and an ice cube, or at the paint easels.
2. Roses—Children paint, watercolor, or food-color coffee filters with different shades of red and pink. Place the filters inside each other and staple to a bulletin board. Create a rosebush effect with varying shades of green tissue paper. Attach brown construction-paper stems.

Music

1. *Beauty and the Beast* cassette by Disney.
2. *Sing Along Songs, Volume 10: Be Our Guest* video by Disney.

Cooking

Fruit Salad

Combine oranges, plums, pineapples, bananas, grapes, pears, and watermelon in a fruit salad for children to sample. All of these fruits appear in the story.

Skewered Fruits

Using fruits that appear in the story, place orange sections, plum chunks, pineapple chunks, banana slices, grapes, pear chunks, and watermelon chunks on skewers in differing orders. Cut a slice from the bottom (stem end) of several oranges, place them on plates and stick the skewers into the oranges. Let one child name one fruit from the above list, and students (who have been supplied with forks) may then remove that fruit from their skewers to eat—but only if it is the piece on the end. Continue the game, selecting a different person to name the next piece of fruit until all have had a turn and all fruit desired is eaten.

Game

Beauty and the Beast Magic Mirror Card Game by Parker Brothers (a delightful matching game).

Video

Beauty and the Beast by Disney

Beauty and the Beast

Story Web

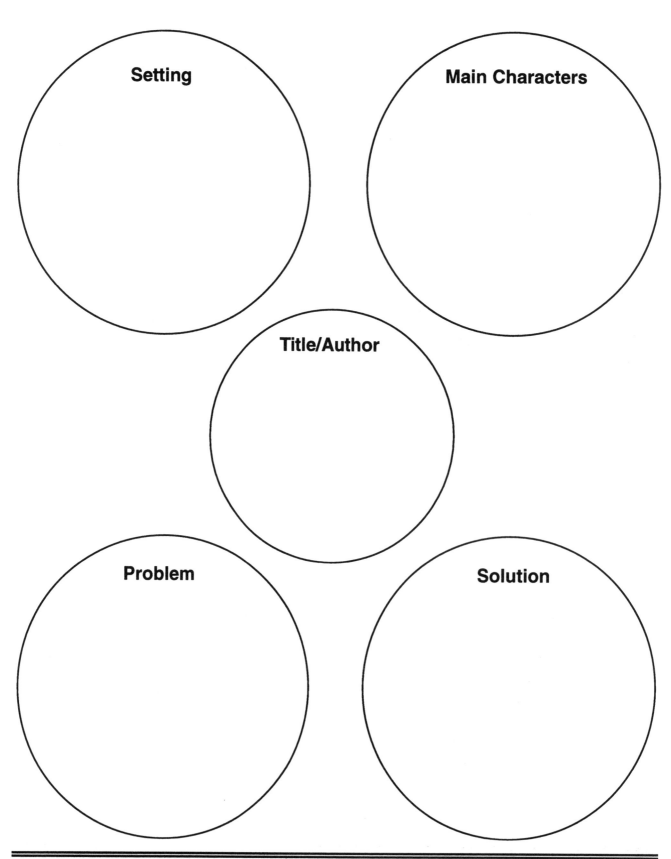

Setting

Main Characters

Title/Author

Problem

Solution

Venn Diagram
(to compare and contrast stories, ideas, or characters)

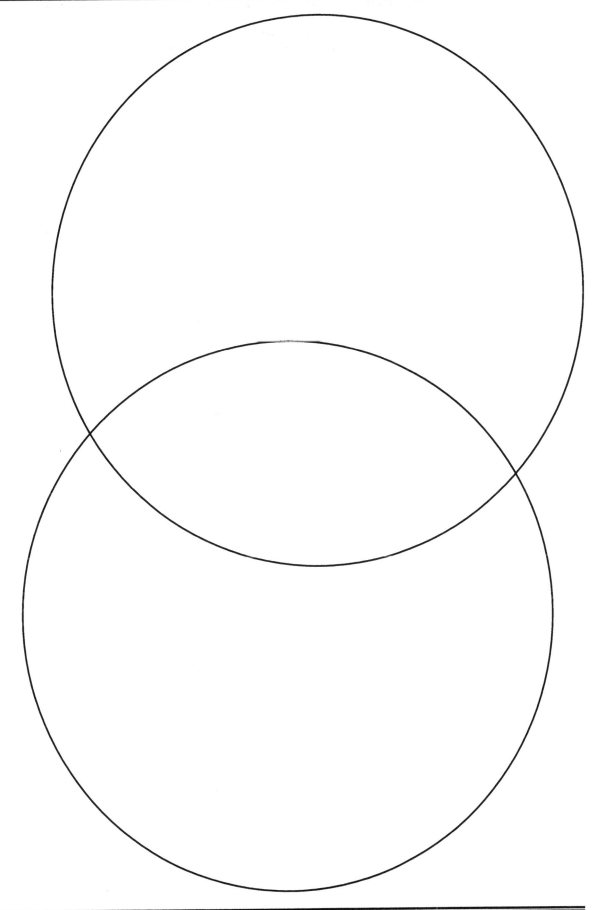

© 1995 Teacher Created Materials, Inc.   #454 Favorite Authors: Jan Brett

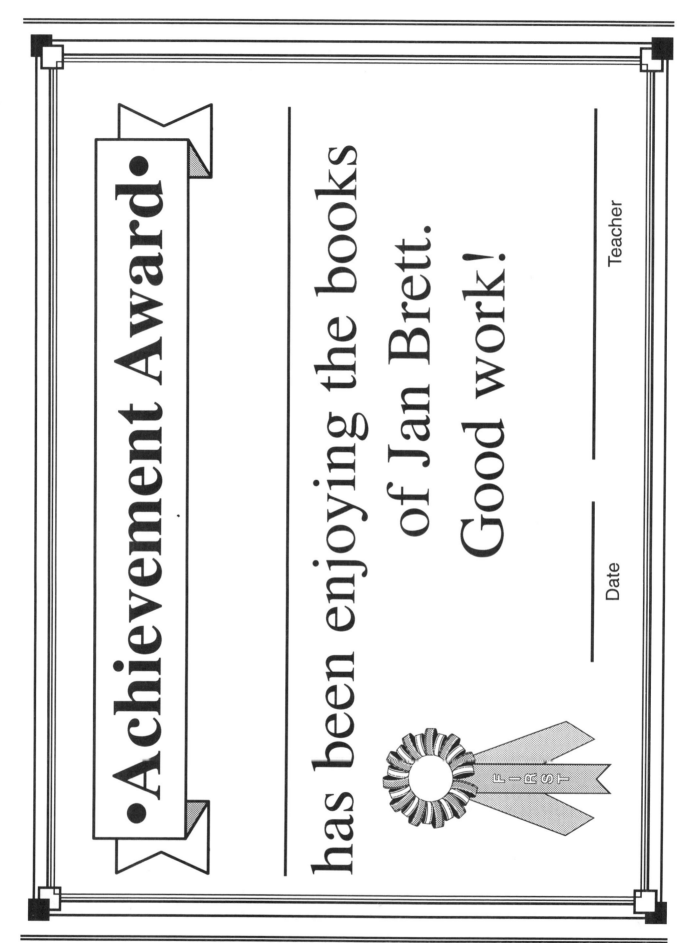

Materials and Resources

The Best of the Mailbox, Preschool/Kindergarten
    The Education Center, Inc.
    1607 Battleground Ave.
    Greensboro, NC 27408
    1-800-334-0298

Childhood
    8873 Woodbank Drive
    Bainbridge Island, WA 98110
    (206) 842-3472
    (for *Goldilocks and the Three Bears* wooden magnet story set)

Gallaudet University Bookstore
    800 Florida Ave. N.E. B2OE
    Washington, DC 20002
    (202) 651-5380
    (for "I Love You" cookie cutter and *Sign Me a Story Video* for *Goldilocks and the Three Bears,*
    Little Red Riding Hood, and other sign language materials and supplies)

Scholastic Book Club
    1-800-325-6149
    (Jan Brett author center with interview cassette)

She Sells Sea Shells
    1157 Periwinkle Way
    Sanibel Island, FL 33957
    (813) 472-6991
    (offers a wide selection of seashells to use with *The Owl and the Pussycat)*

Sugar Sign Press
    1407 Fairmont St.
    Greensboro, NC 27403
    (for sign language information and materials)

Totline
    Warren Publishing House, Inc.
    P.O. Box 2250
    Everett, WA 98203
    (This preschool magazine is published bi-monthly. Subscription rate: $24 year.)

Totline Theme-A-Saurus
    Warren Publishing House, Inc.
    P.O. Box 2250
    Everett, WA 98203

Wildlife Education, Ltd.
    P.O. Box 85271, Suite 6
    San Diego, CA 92138
    1-800-334-8152

(*Zoobook* subscription: $15.95 for 10 issues. Individual bear, dinosaur, and owl *Zoobooks* may be purchased at teacher's supply stores or children's book stores.)

© 1995 Teacher Created Materials, Inc.   *# 454 Favorite Authors: Jan Brett*

Materials and Resources *(cont.)*

Books

Bailey, Jill. *Discovering Rats and Mice.* Bookwright Press, 1987.

Cheltenham Elementary School Kindergartners. *We Are All Alike . . . We Are All Different.* Scholastic, 1991.

Guarino, Deborah. *Is Your Mama a Llama?* Scholastic, 1989.

Jeffers, Susan. *All the Pretty Horses.* Macmillan, 1974.

Nelson, Esther L. *Musical Games for All Ages.* Sterling Publishing Co., Inc., 1976.

Turkle, Brinton. *Deep in the Forest.* E.P. Dutton, 1976.

Watts, Barrie. *Honeybees.* Englewood Cliffs, Silver Burdett, 1989.

Records

Musical Munkins. *The Musical Munkins Are...Makin' Music.*

> Musical Munkins, Inc.
> P.O. Box 356
> Pound Ridge, NY 10576
> (914) 764-8568

Palmer, Hap. *The Feel of Music.*

_____. *Homemade Band.*

_____. *Sally the Swinging Snake.*

> Educational Activities, Inc.
> Box 392
> Freeport, NY 11520

Raffi. *Raffi's Christmas Album.*

> A & M Records
> P.O. Box 118
> Hollywood, CA 90028

Sharon, Lois and Bram. *One Elephant, Deux Elephants.*

> Elephant Records
> P.O. Box 101
> Station 7
> Tor, Canada M5N 2Z3

Weisman, Miss Jackie. *Sniggles, Squirrels, and Chicken Pox.*

> Miss Jackie Music Company
> 10001 El Monte
> Overland Park, KS 66207